Perhaps Bag

Perhaps Bag

Carol Rumens

Sheep Meadow Press
Rhinebeck, New York

Designed and typeset by The Sheep Meadow Press
Distributed by The University Press of New England

Cover image: Vassily Kandinsky
Author Photograph: by Rebecca Rumens

Second Printing
Library of Congress Cataloging-in-Publication Data

Names: Rumens, Carol, author.
Title: Perhaps bag / Carol Rumens.
Description: Rhinebeck, NY : Sheep Meadow Press, [2017]
Identifiers: LCCN 2016051292 | ISBN 9781937679712 (pbk.)
Classification: LCC PR6068.U6 P47 2017 | DDC 823/.914--dc23
LC record available at https://lccn.loc.gov/2016051292

All inquiries and permission requests should be addressed to the publisher:

The Sheep Meadow Press
PO Box 84
Rhinebeck, NY 12514

Sheep Meadow Press thanks Rumens' UK publishers; The Emma Press, Seren, Bloodaxe, Blackstaff Press, Quartet, Ulsterman, Secker & Warburg, and Chatto & Windus. We thank them for their kind accommodation.

THE PERHAPS-BAG

(The avoska or 'perhaps-bag' was a stretchable string bag used in Soviet Russia when there were food shortages: the name derives from the Russian adverb, 'avos', meaning 'perhaps' or 'hopefully'.

As long as you lived, I carried an *avoska,*
my hope, however glum,
the shops, however haunted.
In every queue, it was the same:
I missed the special offer by a whisker
but found myself presented
with a glut of dead bread-rolls.
I'd rush home, tripping over
the trinkets and lost souls
raining through everyone's sieve,
and light the stove.
I lived for your simple waiting
(one fragment less of myself),
a joke ('good catch!'), your sudden appetite,
the gleaming which unwraps
fresh bread and fills the shelf,
and every ragged hole of the *perhaps.*

Contents

from UNCOLLECTED POEMS (1968–81) AND A STRANGE GIRL IN BRIGHT COLOURS (1973)

from SELECTED POEMS (1987)

from Aztec Sacrifices

from A Necklace of Mirrors (1978)

from Unplayed Music (1981)

from STAR WHISPER (1983)

from DIRECT DIALING (1985)

from THE GREENING OF THE SNOW BEACH (1988)

ICONS, WAVES (1986)

from FROM BERLIN TO HEAVEN (1989)

from THINKING OF SKINS (1993)

from BEST CHINA SKY (1995)

from HOLDING PATTERN (1998)

from HEX (2002)

from NEW POEMS (2004)

from BLIND SPOTS (2008)

from De Chirico's Threads (2010)

Sonnets from Ice and Fire

from Animal People (2016)

from **Bezdelki (2017)**

New, Unpublished Poems (2017)

from **Uncollected Poems** (1968-81)

and

A Strange Girl in Bright Colours (1973)

ADVICE BEFORE THE ACT

The cat's
a real live raver of a
crazy hot-hipped all-girl go-girl   wow
she's fizz-fizz-fizzing over   hey you
nu-type super doll with the EYES ARE
IN look   hit the charts WHAM make it
front-page and punchline flash-snapped over
Soho swinging those sheerest-joy legs
sky high   honey you've switched on heaven
for that aston-martin-ad-boy showing you
his plastic fantastic split-level swing-pad   you're
so wantable   and today there's no
bad odour no mess no strings and all
but all the go-wild-go-to-bed-
in-nothing honeys do it   only don't
slip up will you   always take
that twenty-one day precaution   there's a pill
to medicare your passion   if you
conceive you know
you die?

POST-WAR PORTRAIT

This morning the city has drowned in mist,
thick, plush, elderberry mist that might have poured
from a ghostly reunion of troop-trains.
Poppy-sellers splash the station forecourt.

A woman crossing the glistening street
between buses is mist-coloured too
with her long damp hair and inky denims.
On the train between home and work she read Chekhov,

or gazed out at the adolescent day
in its pinkish drowse, dreaming of many disguises.
Now she vies with the impatient traffic,
her mind a rainstorm of words.

How easy, she thinks, for poems to be born in gutters.
She'd like to be the eternal student,
her life always in flux, a stream of questions
to which there are countless answers.

Instead, she's supposed to be on time,
earn money, explain things
and be useful, as the years
etch fragments of dark into her senses.

But still she thinks how age might set her free,
cutting the strings her children strain at, how
she'll fly as well. Already, in her city,
there's the stirring of wet, iridescent wings.

One day, she'll travel like the mist,
or lean on steps, idle as a wreath of poppies.
One day, the heavy magnets of her love
will be tiny, piercing, star-like memories

and immortality will claim her
if she can only keep the sharp cold throbbing
in her bones, the blue November clouds
rushing beneath her feet.

SPANISH FUNFAIR

What armies of magic children,
helmets clamped above starry eyes
pulled this pagan trompe l'oeil
out of the skull-capped mountain?
What fanciful strategist still
skims the cable-car lanterns
over the precipice into the diesel-blue
of a Barcelona matins,
and sweeps them back to the crag,
shaken with pride; who launches
the little red 'plane into nowhere
and back? It slows on its flight path,
and is mobbed by the infant jet-set.
This is the paradise dreamed
by hand-cranked, rusting horses
shambling around some corner of forever,
runningboards free for a day
to the swifter shoeless. If
there's a terrible key, arms braced
at the heart of the innocence, we
forget. Like a judgment suspended,
we float in our cabins, good kings
of the cloudy pine-tops, bound, so the signposts say,
for the Enchanted Castle.

FOLK SONG

Left school a no one
With nothing to keep me
From now to the tomb—

A no-life for no one
And my grey mother moaning
There's work to do at home.

The wheel wasn't turning,
The lift-shaft was empty.
Dad walked in front of me.
He was going home.

I stood on the platform,
The trains ran round me.
Two eyes found me
And took me home.

I dyed my hair.
I opened my window.
A smile stood beside me:
You're wasted at home.

If the grey days moan
There's lights in the Palais
So stuff your untogether
Old dole and doom.

I'll marry in leather
When I'm thirty-three
And nearly in the tomb.

My face will save me,
My savings befriend me.
My life will spend me
And chuck me in a home.

OBJECTS AND SHADOWS

Before their time, the child-red apples crown,
Birthmarked with gold. We have no child like these
Under the sun. We visit empty-handed.
In dark leaf-nests the children swarm and fatten.

Hard-fleshed desires surround these celibate nights:
Nights of gold wine, red flowers and dishes, sweetened
Out of the limitless artistry of hunger,
Not to be tried: nights of the nerveless conscience;
Nights of well-chosen words passed without fumbling,

Electrifying the tiny wire between
Host and guest, mourner and ghost. We pause
For the last time at a first imperfect kiss.
To see, to touch, to hold, to possess:
The infinitives multiply on the merciless tree.
Foresight refused to alter this, could not
Turn back the diver from his pool of flame,
Nor warn the desperate climber to renounce
The glimpse of burning apples, far or falling,
Falling absurd, untasted into winter.

LATEST MODEL

I've been trying for years
to get him right. I scrapped
the old loud-mouthed straight-liner—
durable but inapt
for the subtleties of his mistress.
This one's much finer.
When I call him from paradise,
when I hide my presence in
his brow, his lovely eyes,
he appears to listen and look;
he answers pertinently.
He's also an excellent cook
and cares about his skin.
Where did I ruin him?
It's not that badge of assertive
appetite he wears
in the shadows of his thighs.
It's not that he satisfies it
too quickly or too coldly
(though sometimes he does).
It's not that he tends to vote
for the party with guns and money
(though he's fond of both).
I don't know what it is.
He's my best animal,
the bright crown of my skill:
I know him, and know nothing.
For hours I sit at his side,
invisibly praising him,
smoothing his discontents,

enumerating his talents,
stroking sleek his pride.
With all my creatorly will
I breathe and breathe on him,
yet something insensate, wood,
stays put, fails to get warm.
I think he's afraid
to imagine me beyond
some carved thing he has made.
I'd smash it if I dared:
but how can one artist harm
the work of another's hands?
I already feel how he'll grieve
when I die of his failure to live.

MAUREEN'S MAGNIFICAT

You were called Maureen, aged five
And chosen to play the Virgin
Because of your long red hair.
I thought it a little unfair—
You weren't even coached or tried—
But you looked so perfectly right
For the part, I had to forgive you.
All the house went hushed at the sight
Of the flamey stream that fell
Down the back of your sky-blue shift
As you knelt so still, so still
And the Angel mumbled: 'Fear not.'

Nothing else about you was rare,
You were squat, with a broad pink face
And pale eyes that seemed puzzled
By the rumour of your hair.
It was down to your waist by now.
You must have moaned when your mother's
Stiff, stout brush raked out
The sparkling knots, and on Friday
Nights, when she crowned you with foam
And it toppled down over your brows,
You must have shed scalding tears.
But at last she taught you to care.
You began to own your hair.

By the fifth form you'd grown tall.
You sat at the front of the class.
You were not very popular

Nor clever at anything much
Except having long red hair
Which you wore in a rope-thick plait, like a dare.

Nobody bothered to pull it.
Plaits, and you, were right out.
We had perms, we mocked you, no doubt.
Our laughter died that day you unravelled your hair.
Oh, you were more woman than any of us were.

You left school, your life
Knotted up in your red silk hair.
It must have been heavy at times.
You must have felt lonely and small,
High in your tower, locked,
And the boys all crying below,
'Maureen, Maureen, let down your hair!'
What a miracle when you did.
It rose like a twisty stair,
And the bravest one found you there,
Waiting with wide, troubled eyes
For his tender, evasive 'fear nots'.

JUST EVE

Money can buy me love, it's true and terrible.
There's a swirl of colour in the air, spotlights
shaping my desire on every clothes-rail.
The DJ whispers loudly, like a wicked
uncle, gifts and bargains, into every
delicate ear, but any minute now
the songs will start again, and it'll be
real pain stabbing through the fan-whirl:
Stay with me, baby, please, stay with me, baby.
Pink and grey, a dress like petals fondles
my hand and slips. The price-tag
nestles inside me like a chip of glass:
I'm poorer than the pavement. Only money
would make me gleam until he couldn't doubt it,
and I not doubt myself, bringing him
slow flowers across the office, pink and grey.

AT PUBERTY

After rain
a blue light settled over the convent arches;

the naked asphalt astonished itself with diamonds;
even the washed-out plaster virgin
in the Bernadette Grotto, and the mulberry tree
propped up and barren of silkworms,
stepped cleanly out of their decay.

From the back of the music lesson
a girl stared through a window
watching beam upon beam of realisation
incise the long mists of her childhood.

Her thirteenth spring
was born among the tattered pages
of the Older Children's Song Book.

Komme liebe Mai

sang the class, uneasily.
A new emotion, innocent, classical,
yet making her shake and burn,
was softly unravelled
by the clear-eyed woman who sat

at the black Bosendorffer
with her coquettishness and her merciless
gentle arpeggios.

The elm leaves turned, silver-backed,
on a wind coarse as hunger,

and nuns in their distant sanctuary,
the dark-blue brides of Christ,
closed their ears to the sin, the soft
tired alto of girls at puberty;
heard still a child's soprano.

O impossible miracles, light
out of straggle-rowed chairs
and school-room floor-boards—

the girl, pale as clouds,
stares for a year, aching
at the vision which has no need
of the speechless peasant,

which will suddenly vanish, leaving
only the deep river between them—

the woman who needed nothing,
and the child who promised everything.

ME-TIME

Been interviewing my latest grin all day,
but still smell daisy-fresh—a nice, tall boy

in a roll-neck shirt, John Stephen's aubergine,
who watches on the monitor again

that grin flashing through legends of trendiness.
Wheels spin, there's a girl in my Lotus, the smile speeds west,

swerves, brakes, and now it's on my face.
Somebody coughs. Relax. They love to hate.

All things bright and beautiful are fake
and that means me. Just hear those punch-lines make

the laughter-scene. Style mod, intentions trad—
that's what they dig. I pray. Calm down. A hand,

folks, cos I'm proud to have for our next guest
a movie-star who's quit the Wild West

for Vietnam. What's his name? O yes. Hi there,
James Henry. Tell us, what's it like, this war?

Uh huh. The hawks wear doves now? Want to win
only to pack up fighting and go home?

That's great news. Great. The loud-mouth's overrun.
No kid? That's great. Where did I put my pun?

Well thanks a lot for talking. That was great.
I'm sorry. Once again our time's run out.

I'm sweating. Thar's his best Vietnam thumbs-up.
'You're a pro,' he says. I am? 'I wish you luck.'

THE ADVANCED SET

My three mysterious uncles
were my father's elder brothers,
but not like him at all.

Arranged in steps, by age,
their three small portraits frowned
above the tea-time doilies.

They didn't frown at me,
but as if they sensed
each other's eyes, too close.

My grandma, sawing bread,
glanced back at them before telling
how they cook care not to speak

when, by an oversight,
they were in the house together.
They ate in relays.

What did they do next?
They went to war. One
got taken prisoner.

(His tortured shadow lurked
dark yellowish in the damp stain
behind the print of Mount Fuji.)

One lived by the sea.
He had asthma and a mistress.
The other drank port-wine,

alone and grand in Tonbridge,
officer class to the end.
Without a word they slipped

past my childhood gaze,
having never patted my head
or spun me a sixpence.

Those three Advanced Level uncles—
complex as love affairs,
far as the Burma Road—

might have talked to me in the end
but had the wit to die
before I grew tall enough

to sweep the brown photos down,
laugh at them, dance on them,
sigh, 'But you're ordinary.'

A POSTCARD FROM BRIGHTON, 1980

One man's whelk is another's cornucopia.
Jeremy Treglown

Now there's nothing—
only a mad blue wall
building and toppling itself
hopelessly, over and over,
in the cage it can't understand.
We sit down suddenly like babies,
and stare at our cuttlefish shins.
Everything ends here—
the Victorian wrought-iron
descending in pastel-green waves,
the sound of feet munching
the land's dish of leftovers;
the railway, and the pink tickets
always nearly lost—
even London ends here,
signing itself off
in dots of panicky neon.
We are locked in the mad blue present,
an instamatic snap
from the eye of some child, a king.
His palace, a harem of curves,
glitters behind us; his artists
are now at work on the sky.
The real children have bought
a beach-scene to send home,
saying Don't you wish you were here?
They scan the polished crescent
of *pointilliste* sunbathers,

and readily pick themselves out,
so confident are they
that their particular gladness,
shadelessly gold and blue,
finds its true place in this.

APRIL IN FEBRUARY

(for Becky)

At four, the afternoon's baby eye
is opened still—a miracle. The blue
fades slowly in my bare, west-facing window.
Its lingering is as sweet and new as April—
when folk still long to go on pilgrimages
through the old dust of houses, marriages—
your month. You wailed in that municipal
ward, in your pollen-coloured Babygro . . .
Birth tunes us sharp and makes us fall in love.
Then we must live with it. These days, you change
faster than the year, or seem unchanged,
depending on my light. Think of the downs—
still in their thick, tucked, winter pelt of mud:
small birds, circling on the air's lasso,
over and over each black, thorny crown,
find nothing creeping or unfurling there.
Yet if we walked towards them now, I believe
the hills would be all softly green and scattered
with those faint suns, those small, tremendous wishes—
primroses of April, of your month.

NOVEMBER

The wind is sudden.
Leaves pass like millennia
rusting the hill.
One by one, the trees
will open to let in light,
each twig a small seed-fern,
a fossil of the air.

from **Selected Poems** (1987)

THE LAST DAY OF MARCH

The elms are darkened by rain.
On the small, park-sized hills
Sigh the ruined daffodils
As if they shared my refrain—
That when I leave here, I lose
All reason to see you again.

What's finishing was so small,
I never mentioned it.
My time, like yours, was full,
And I would have blushed to admit
How shallow the rest could seem;
How so little could be all.

FALSE WINGS

The house with its many windows drew the dawn
into itself, and light touched open shapes
and colours—a yellow quilt, our human darkness.
Pillow-grass flowered in all its varieties—
your lashes, soft as charrings, the crisp maze
curling along each forearm,
tiny needles of midnight in your jaw.
By the day's slow brightening,
I discovered the clairvoyance of your eyelids.
They flickered up, even before my lips
had found your sleeping face.
I loved your look of happiness, its pure welcome.
You touched me like your first-born, with a marvelling
sweetness that inventoried each part
and found me whole; yet you touched my heart
most when, climbing our tumult, you took its peak
with a child's candour, and I saw my name
flying out of the sun, amazed by falling.

SIMPLE POEM

Why didn't the room say
how long your absence would be,
that night when you climbed the stairs
in your quick, expectant way
and sat across from me?
No word from the lamp or the chair
though they've both been around a bit
and ought to have guessed, not a sign
from the much-used willow plate.
It watched you laugh and eat
and did not seem to care,
as lost in desire as I—
and now you're not here.

And now you're not here, why
must there still be a room
with surfaces that mime
the slow life of the sky,
and a clock to strike off time?
Like an implacable heart
the blind swings open, shut,
on leafy blue, on grey.

Darkness refuses to stay,
and always the numb dawn light
shows a chair, raggedly turned,
and a small lamp that once burned
all through the summer night.
Oh, how the light loved then
all the white length of your spine.
My pillow was dark with your hair.
Why doesn't everything die
now you're not here?

BALLAD OF THE MORNING AFTER

Take back the festive midnight,
Take back the sad-eyed dawn:
Wind up that old work ethic.
Oh, let me be unborn.

After a night of travelling,
How can it come to pass
That there's the same tongue in my mouth
The same face in my glass,

Same light on the curtain,
Same thirst in the cup,
Same ridiculous notion
Of never getting up?

Cars stream above the city;
The subway throbs below,
Whirling a million faces
Like shapeless scraps of snow,

And all these melting faces
Flying below and above
Think they are loved especially
Think they especially love.

This is a free country.
The jails are for the bad:
The only British dissidents
Are either poor or mad.

I put my classless jeans on,
Open my lockless door;
I breathe the air of freedom
And know I'm mad and poor.

Love is the creed I grew by,
Love is the liberal's drug—
Not Agape but Eros
With his Utopian hug

And in the *close, supportive*
Environment of the bed,
He is liberty, equality,
Fraternity and bread.

That is the supposition—
But I say love's a joke,
A here-today-and-gone-tomorrow
Childish pinch-and-poke.

Perhaps I'll believe in something
Like God or Politics;
I'd build those temples wider
But there are no more bricks.

Some women believe in Sisterhood;
They've rowed the Master's ship
Across the lustful silver sea
On his last ego-trip,

And some believe in Housework,
And a few believe in Men.
There's only one man that I want,
And I want him again and again.

He sat down at my table.
He finished all the wine.
'You're nothing, dear, to me,' he said,
But his body covered mine,

And stoked the fiery sickness
That's done me to a turn—
The fool that chose to marry
And also chose to burn.

Burning burning burning
I came to self-abuse,
Hoping I'd go blind, but no,
It wasn't any use.

I see a mother and her child
Both turn with starving face.
And that's the story of our lives,
The whole damned human race.

My conscience is a hangover,
My sex-life, chemistry;
My values are statistics,
My opinions, PMT.

Beside my rented window
I listen to the rain.
Yes, love's a ball of iron,
And time, its short, sharp chain.

The middle-aged say life's too brief.
The old and young say 'wrong'.
I'll tell you, if you don't like life,
It's every day too long.

CARPET WEAVERS, MOROCCO

The children are at the loom of another world.
Their braids are oiled and black, their dresses bright.
Their assorted heights would make a melodious chime.

They watch their flickering knots like television.
As the garden of Islam grows, the bench will be raised.
Then they will lace the dark-rose veins of the tree-tops.

The carpet will travel in the merchant's truck.
It will be spread by the servants of the mosque.
Deep and soft, it will give when heaped with prayer.

The children are hard at work in the school of days.
From their fingers the colours of all-that-will-be fly
and freeze into the frame of all-that-was.

A NEW SONG

(for Naim Attallah)

> *Thou feedest them with the bread of tears;*
> *and givest them tears to drink in great measure.*
> PSALM 90

Silences of old Europe
Not even the shofar
Can utter: Maidenek,
Mauthausen, Babi Yar—

Death of the innocent being
Our speciality
Let us add Lebanon's breaking
Sob to the litany.

So many now to mourn for,
Where can the psalmist start?
Only from where his home is,
And his untidy heart.

We pluck our first allegiance
With a curled baby-hand,
Peering between its fingers
To see our promised land;

Yours on a hillside, clouded
With olives; mine a cot
In a London postal district,
Its trees long spilled as soot.

The war was all but over:
It seems my newborn cry
Was somehow implicated
In yells of victory.

But it's the quieter voices
That keep on trying to rhyme,
Telling me almost nothing,
But filling me with shame:

Germany in the thirties
And half my family tree
Bent to an SS microscope's
Mock genealogy.

Duly pronounced untainted
For his Aryan bride,
My uncle says it's proven—
There are no Jews on our side.

Ancient, unsummoned, shameless,
The burdens of prejudice:
All through my London childhood,
Adults with kindly eyes

Muttered the mild opinions
So innocently obscene
(Hitler was not 'all stupid',
and 'not all Jews are mean').

Later, the flickering movie;
Greyish, diaphanous
Horrors that stared and questioned:
Has God forgotten us?

Oh, if our unborn children
Must go like us to flame,
Will you consent in silence,
Or gasp and burn with them?

It is so late in the century
And still the favourite beast
Whines in the concrete bunker
And still the trucks roll east

And east and east through whited
Snowfields of the mind
Towards the dark encampment;
Still the Siberian wind

Blows across Prague and Warsaw,
The voices in our head
Baying for a scapegoat:
Historians gone mad;

Thugs on a street corner,
The righteous gentile who
Pins Lebanon like a yellow star
To the coat of every Jew.

Silences of old Europe
Be broken; let us seek
The judgement of the silenced,
And ask how they would speak.

Then let the street musician
Crouched in the cruel sun
Play for each passing, stateless
Child of Babylon,

Conciliatory harmonies
Against the human grain,
A slow psalm of two nations
Mourning a common pain—

Hebrew and Arabic mingling
Their single-rooted vine;
Olives and roses falling
To sweeten Palestine.

ASHQELON

At Ashqelon, I searched
a diaspora of sea-shells
for the perfect affinities
of size and patterning
that make a couple.

Little hinged bivalves,
they were unpartnered now.
Marked out for loneliness
as faces are,
each knew its sad uniqueness.

The sea had never valued
their delicate compacts.
It had plunged them into war,
then dragged them, fighting and broken,
and beaten them into the shore.

There they lay, one nation,
bathed in a flickering dream
which every sleeper read
from his own eyelids.
And, as I gazed at them,

it was as if the sea
scattered them still, or the wind,
and whirled their coloured rain
to the ends of Ashqelon,
and to shores that have no end.

AT KIBBUTZ AMIAD

These are the solid texts—
houses in white lanes
scribbled with jacaranda.
But it's in the margins

we'll find our poems
said footloose Mandelstam.
I weigh this as you sleep
and all the kibbutzim

of the Upper Galilee
grow moody with children
escaping vaguely home,
tired as the khamsin.

Quarrels, piano practice—
nothing is lonelier
in this story of families
than our marginalia .

We keep ourselves to ourselves
in a flower-shadowed house
with an empty second bedroom
that cannot fathom us.

ECLIPSES

Midday. The earth holds its breath,
the shadows can't move an inch.
Only the sky seems to be rushing away.
It vanishes into the blue of its furthest blue,
dropping a little curled handful of sun-smeared iris
onto the world for us.
The poppies are clear glass bowls of some inky night-cap,
the grass, an amazement of light.
And you and I, what are we,
our soft, random collision
eclipsing us in this garden,
this room? Pass your hand
quickly over the sun's brow and invent
a glowing midday dusk
where I shall undress to my ear-studs
and you, to nothing. Where the exotic, slow,
brachiating animal we evolve,
time-lapsed, will have no name,
and I'll press my lips by mistake to my own skin.

IN THE CRAFT MUSEUM

Some nations lock up their poets. Ours have the key
To a high, clean room labelled Sensibility.

They have sat there now for a very long time,
And are clearly no threat to a democratic regime.

They are old, of course, but remarkably unspoiled;
Their edges still cut, their moving parts are oiled.

Of course, they're permitted to go down to the street,
And the street may visit them, if it wipes its feet.

Here comes the guide now, telling the solemn young faces
That, yes, the poets still work, but don't touch the glass cases.

WEST BERLIN PASTORAL

Hans's country retreat
was a few minutes drive from Head Office,
but country, nevertheless.

If we weren't quite at ease,
neither was our taciturn host,
born on that side of the Wall

where nobody would splash graffiti
to make themselves immortal.
There were too many tongues, adrift

and tipsy with cross-currents,
for one simple picnic;
but the grass befriended us,

and the thick gooseberry hedge
that marked the boundary
between the woods, birch-misted,

and our luminous clearing, dropped
its sweets into our palms.
Someone began 'Kalinka'

and Hans joined in, loudly
word-perfect, commandeering
the drama of its *tempo rubato*.

The sweat broke on his brow
like raw grain; we could tell
he had learned success

at the knees of the Komsomol.
When the small fire-roses
had faded in the charcoal,

and the flats and sandy shallows
of a mildly remarkable sunset
flooded darkly over,

he lit the hurricane lamps
ranged along the privy roof,
and ordered us to dance.

Then, with a slight sigh,
he sat back watching us,
his feet in their triple-striped

yellow Adidas jumping
on the overturned beer-crate
like two insane bees.

We were babbling nightingales now,
paired and cradled and brilliant
with impromptu history.

Drunk, we knew every language,
and that every language was touch,
every wall, a gooseberry bush.

THE COMPASS PLANT

Ya skuchayu pa tehye.

'I am bored without you'
is Russian for 'I miss you',
but somehow weightier:
east of the Brandenburg Gate,

boredom can be very black.
It gets a whole mouthful of sounds
with a cruel twist at the end
like something Fate might do.

It resembles 'escutcheon'—
a bat-like museum-piece,
solid, medieval, filthy
with a coat-of-arms we can't read,

declaring the thickness of blood.
Bored as a sentry I've taken
to vodka and dictionaries.
I guzzle words like a fly-trap,

but am really a compass plant,
my leaves tracking the sun
with blades perpendicular
to the incoming light,

irreversibly orientated
to you, your tongue, your absence.
If I seem to be asleep,
my senses are open wide;

I am highly photoperceptive,
and geared to the trembliest rumour.
All future-tense, I dream
bored into borders, opened.

LOVERS IN WESTGATE GARDENS

When I passed them, tucked away
On a bench cut deep into the privet,

I observed two masculine hands at urgent play
On a small, cotton-clad, feminine ribcage,

Which seemed content to lie there and accept
The attention, snug and close as a bird in its plumage.

At once your absence swept me, fiery-cold,
And common envy, spiteful, mean and dull,

Froze to my skin. I thought how, when we loved,
I could do something better than lie still.

Then a sharp rustling shook the dark-leafed bower;
The lovers faded, you sat quietly waiting

For me to notice you, to sense you'd spoken.
'In love, the one pleased has no less power

Than the one who pleases. To accept with grace
Is also to give.' And then, it seemed, you opened

Your arms towards me so consentingly,
I was enfolded in that mystery.

SECOND LIVES

Wedging himself by degrees
through the unlatched door,
the foundling tomcat

with his double set of neuroses
looks at the woman in bed,
decides he needn't leave.

They listen to the plug
knuckling the wall's far side,
then the granular buzz

of coffee-beans spinning
into fragments of themselves,
truer than themselves.

Around her stand the dead,
risen as usual,
encumberings of teak

veneer, uncut moquette,
thin brass and sprigged plastic
glooming in the dawn

of her second life.
The man who left that crumpled
space on her right,

chose them carefully.
She knows in which junk-shops
and at what price.

He was by himself,
breathing in the strong essence
of private ownership,

tongue-tied and stateless
as the tense face that dodged him
from mirror to speckled mirror.

This is his second country;
she, his lost wives;
she is twenty, thirty, forty

as she waits for him to bring
the Oxfam tray
with its dusty wicker plait

and scribble of poppies.
He'll set it gently down
on the quilt's collapsing flesh,

and, stepping back to watch
her childish pleasure, taste
the day's first sip with her.

DARK HARVEST

They shine like tiny apples, black,
Scented with gin and loneliness,
The easiest fruit, perhaps, to pick
But firm against my tongue's duress
As I interrogate their skin
Kindly, tactfully, knowing that soon
They'll have to break, confess their lies
Of ripeness till my whole mouth cries.

A bush of fruit-lamps burns as clear
In Harrow as in Chistopol.
It brings the life you fled so near
I'm dizzy with its taste and smell.
I wade breast-deep, the whispering bush
Opening up, against my wish,
Those glints and lights I least can bear—
The darkest eyes, the softest hair.

They have survived their altered state,
Your exiled loves. They stir their tea
With teaspoon-clouds of summer fruit,
And test the sweetness patiently.
Your absence falls as light as dust,
Now, on the lives. They're almost used
To swallowing what's dull and cruel:
I think they almost wish you well.

CHRISTMAS DINNER BORSCHT

Don't look for spies or angels in our kitchen.
We're Christmas-ing far from all religions.
Utopia doesn't mean a thing to us,
And we've forgotten how to talk to children.

Eating, though, continues. And ever since
I dipped my spoon into this wavy, scarlet
Winter sun, lifted its cap of beet-leaves,
I've felt as festive as a wedding taxi

Climbing in clouds of exhaust, frost, ribbons,
With a bride who'll simply giggle and take snaps.
The sandy, pointed beard, implacably growthless
In its mausoleum, needn't expect a visit.

Don't look for revolution. In our kitchen
We know religions all get cooked and eaten.
And artists catch only the incarnation,
Its living wonder, kissed from Rheims to Kiev.

Cooks, too, like colour. Look, our beetroot angels
Were here before us, bowed towards our plates.
They've left their traces, though the soup has vanished:
For each of us, one rose-gold halo print!

from **Aztec Sacrifices**

EXILES

Who lives in this city, this beached raft
of half-dried lake where the world's skin
splits when God frowns, and churches topple?
Far off, the grass is floating, flowery punts
moving funereal into river mist,
and here the city nomads shadow panes
lit with 'Tacos y Tortas', stripes of airlines.
Who looks for Anahuac? Who tries for a foothold?

. . . Your worklords, Lebanese millionaires, basking
in a sheen of glass and gold carpets,
their pleasure boat on the waters of Babylon;
the maids in the supermarket,
each with a small, white child in a wire trolley,
patiently clearing paths through a world of short weight;

we, deserting Gringos, circling each other
under the cypresses of the Noche Triste;
the orange-seller, crouched all day on his blanket;
street-corner cops, teeth glittering at bribes;
scorpions; the government in its white
armed mansion . . . But who will moor this city
in his own rootage? Whom does the city cradle?

A SONG OF EMPIRES

To the bright ports of the East they came,
pirates and tyrants, a spreading stain
on the water they called the Spanish Main
            Soli Deo Gloria.

Their pox-pit mines were the land's disease;
they leached the lakes, silenced the trees,
but the slave-ships sped through the restless seas,
            Soli Deo Gloria.

From Quito and Cuzco they sucked the soul,
and the Inca king has gone blazing to hell;
beneath the white dome lies the begging-bowl
            Soli Deo Gloria.

Their Vera Cruz, a shining gun,
rose again and roared at the sun
until he cracked. The caked wheels spun
            Soli Deo Gloria.

What coins will be banked when the gold is gone,
when the might of the church is a hollow tomb,
who'll marry the dark and the light as one
            Soli Deo Gloria?

The dollar will rule when the viceroys sail,
and the Revolution lie stiff and pale
in the plate-glass kingdoms beyond the jail
            Soli Deo Gloria.

TEZCATLIPOCA AND THE SORCERERS

As we worked our sorceries seawards
into rocks and hurricanes,
we knew he would come to us,
weaving all his colours
and memories to one zigzag
above the Paso de Cortés;
and again we'd call him Lord,
Lord of the Smoking Mirror.
When he dropped level with us,
we smelt bad meat, and tried
not to interpret or notice
the dim lank plume of his headdress
dissolved in glittering fleas.
We tried to take his hands
but his mirrors blazed up, and choked
pity and prayer alike.
His lip plug struggled to fly
as he reprimanded us
in a voice of sand
because we were only priests
who had never jumped in the fire
or lost a foot in battle.
'Those who march now', he whispered,
'march with the heavens behind them.'
And the wheels of the planets groaned
and seemed to run us down.
He fell on his hands among us,
was jaguar, jaguar wounded;
gulped air and tears until
he was muscled and striped and golden,

racing his wound, up and up
into the empty place
where gods die and perhaps
are sometimes born.
So we continued without him
into the war smoke, into the burning mirrors
we needed no god to conjure.

LAS BRISAS

A day after the first mosquito bites
our bodies flare with peso-sized stigmata.
They come between desire and us all night;
our book of dreams grows jumpy with errata.

Guilty, I try to recollect the crime,
and plunge again our river's coiled green flow,
parting the wavering maize and sky-washed palm,
the silk mud streaming from my swimming toe.

The game's to drift away from you, dissolve
in deeper, colder waters, then strike back
full of the thrill and fear I'll never have
earth's warmth again, your coat spread on the bank.

Thirsty towards dusk, we dropped some coins
at a shabby stall for gulps of melon ice.
And the mosquitoes' delicate, piercing rains
visited the rivers of paradise.

QUETZALCOATL

The stone eyes gazing meet the stone eyes gazing.
Quetzalcoatl, phoney, unabashed
municipal folk hero, basks his coils
in ornamental waters, not perhaps

entirely sham, not quite content to cast
his skin of symbols for the latest fashion.
We follow him along the broad lake-path
striped cool with palm, an effortless translation

of Europe into America. Sunday whites
flash at dark throats, the zoo birds flame, but you
lower your eyes. You're sick of cantaloupe
and orchid, the ripe hot-house of my hope,

and I'm unsure of victory when I gaze
at you emblazoned on the sun's fierce gaze,
the heroes' fountains hanging like white fires
above the wood, air sharp with battle cries.

You want your own Independenzia!
Will you kill for it, die for it? I know
the price of parks, this suffering white and green;
I see the tribesman fighting through a rain

of hurled pots to snatch the leaping spring,
and civilisation, like a tiny fish,
glinting in his blind pitcher. Would you fork
new flames across the mellowed paths of conquest?

Angry, you comb your fingers through the serpent's
granite quills. And if we faced each other
now, there'd be no truce, no tail-in-mouth.
The stone eyes gazing meet the stone eyes gazing.

IN THE JARDIN D'ESPAGNE

Two children swing through an ironware jungle
in the Jardin d'Espagne. You're so late
I'm almost out of breath. I try to stare through the trees
into the windowed heart of sub-Manhattan.

Which cube picks out in strip-lit migraine your
tequila-breathing deals and machinations,
or do you service the other wing of the city?
What klaxoning auto breaks your guilty run?

Can two children hold off my madness
with small, stained hands, or the worn toe of a shoe?
The orange slide swoops to white concrete.
Their colours wrestle in a clash of shadows.

Dusk, and the respectable families leave,
but the rusty-horsed roundabout keeps shambling
its sinews like a clock. The city brightens,
ringing our leafy island with pale fire.

Shall I set out towards one of the postcards,
lit with the names that mean money,
or try the high shrilling peaks of Mestizo Spanish,
my tongue already lost like a Nahua text

in the blaze of civilisation? How can I reach you
from a cancelled self? The date trees' shadows
claw the gravel. I am beyond one word.
Please, please, can you tell me—

How do you ask, how do you understand?
I pray to all the lost gods for a trochee singing
out of the dark, my name and my existence
on smiling lips: only the squeak and tick

of the roundabout, and scattered footsteps, answer.
Two children are making a game
of snipers and searchlights. Their bright eyes hold me.
I am in border country, wasteland of spies

and wetbacks, the running shadow, the aimed gun,
motionless, nameless. If I'm still alive
where is my voice, why do the words lie silent
under the scream? Why is the scream silent?

WONDER

When you watch the bird-limbed boy in a celluloid haze,
strung on the rack of his growing and his hunger,
dying an inch, a light-year, from your cable,
remember your children. Wonder at their birth.

When the fatherly general with the strategic smile
despatches flame to some peaceful delta hamlet
and from every child the ground sucks a crimson shadow,
remember your children. Wonder at their birth.

When you count the dead in your heart's comparable desert,
when two stone figures meet without sight or touch
upon the last bright field where love was promised,
remember your children. Wonder at their birth.

And when you bleed in accordance with your season,
in time with the cold moon where men have stood,
congratulate those who escaped becoming human:
remember your children. Wonder at their birth.

TRICKSTERS AND QUETZALS

Grasshopper Park: a lake about to burn
so everything must fly, or try to learn

quickly: trees, bearing their double cross
of leaded silver paint and Spanish moss,

tangerines in untopplable pyramids,
the cartoon carollings, *Feliz Navidads*

trickling down through pumice fog, hot beats
of light from streams of Detroit metal sheets,

fridges on wheels, with pinwheels for propellers,
and balloons in mass-revolt to launch their sellers.

When the side-saddle optimist on the Witch's Hat
(a child or the child's maid) squeals a scarlet

butterfly into the air,
it's a tiny heart set free, or the brilliant last idea

Moctezuma whispered to his sage:
design, he said, a hopping grasshopper-cage:

line it with Huitzilopochtli's golden shit
and lock the hopping Christians up in it.

from **A Necklace of Mirrors**

(1978)

SAPPHO

Alcaeus jewels her icon—'violet-haired,
holy, sweetly-smiling'—a later hand
adds tears like flecks of heterosexual gilt
as Phaon blunders from her lyric flame.
One little push, and she's a woman again,
the dark hair swirling at Leucadia's foot!

Surely she ground her bread on sharper stone,
entering history beneath some stained
old flag of power, Amazonian spark
spurting under the boot of the patriarch?
She sizzles through the mesh sly Phaon trawls,
naming her lovers by an act of choice
as treacherous as talent: in its heat
are fused the stolen verbs—to love, to write.

LI JU-CHEN'S DREAM

A talented woman is not virtuous woman.
Confucius

My thoughts were a thousand fireflies—
they spun towards the grass
and turned at its touch into women
tall as horses, red as brass.

They were wise, their wishes carried
the might of mandarins.
To the Palace of Curving Water
came husbands, lovers, sons.

They knelt before the women,
their ears were pierced with bone,
their feet so tightly bandaged
the silken rags seemed iron.

And they were pale as nightmares
when the lesson was complete.
The stars looked down in wonder
as the warriors left the gate,

hobbling and weeping homewards,
ears jewelled like wasp-hung pears,
while the laughter of their teachers
called through the dark like bells.

SYLVIA PLATH

Scatter my words to Atlantis
or the chill-lipped mills of the sea;
I am full as the Taxcan mountains
for the earth has married me.

Old patriarch dressed in marble,
I've hung your beard on a vine
and thrown your frown to the leopards of sun
that are leashed to my wrist, that are mine.

I've dropped a gleam of water
like a rock, and like a tree,
two heavy, bright-skinned children,
for the earth has opened me.

Blue-stockings with black notebooks
are howling jealousy,
the Sybil chokes on her cobwebs
for the earth has aproned me.

Old patriarch dressed in marble
why does your eye spark still
under the frown of the earth-haired man
who calls my tigers to heel?

His traps are as sweet as brambles
and old as the hills of the sea,
and the wound is deep and perfect
where the earth has married me.

AKHMATOVA IN LENINGRAD

Queuing at the gate of the Kresty,
The whole city hanging in ice
Like jet beads in a paper-weight,
The woman turned to me twice

As if to convince herself
It was mine, this wrecked white face,
Mine too, the song that had measured
Her hopes in warmer days.

The second time her voice
Was like the first seeping of spring
Wrung from the snow-blue lips
Of a mountainous sorrowing.

'Can you write about this?'
She opened her hand to the wall,
To the women, mute, as if
They queued for the price of a star.

She dropped her hand, she shrugged.
Locked out, I tried to guess
If I'd given her bread or a stone
In the burning clasp of my 'yes'.

from **Unplayed Music**

SUBURBAN

Smoke hour. Brown
death of the blue hydrangea.
Gardens of spilled rust.
So the season smudges over

the measured clarifies
of these hill-cut avenues.
Only the houses seem
still sure of who they are,

solid as bottles of milk.
No season alters them.
They exist, they are proof.
Their owners cherish them

and are in turn defined
by white stucco, black
stripes of thirties Tudor,
the cat, the snowy drapes . . .

or are they? Once
I'd have been sure, accusing.
Now I think of eyes
that wait, of quick hands moving

in windows not yet lit,
and words, less brave than money,
lying spilled and incomplete.
No hard-earned roof stands nearer

now, than the rims of stars
pulsing through time and dark.
The cycling schoolgirls laugh
past their parents' fences.

Love flickers to itself
like an unmatched television.
But the neighbours will say nothing.
The priest will bless it and bury it.

BEFORE THESE WARS

In the early days of marriage
my parents go swimming in an empty sea—
cold as an echo, but somehow *theirs*,
for all its restless size.

From the year 1980 I watch them
putting on the foaming lace.
The sun's gold oils slide from their young skin
and hair as they surface

to fling each other handfuls
of confetti—iced tinsel
and tissue, miniature horseshoes
of silver, white poppy petals.

I search their laughter in vain:
no baby twinkles there,
and Hitler has not yet marched on Poland
beyond the cornflower waves

this print shows pewter.
But that the possible happens
eventually, everyone knows . . .
and when they swim away

the unsettled water fills
with shuddery, dismantled weddings,
a cloud unfurled like an oak tree,
time twisting as it burns.

OVER THE BRIDGE

Cowboys, free-rangers of the late-night bus routes,
they're on the town again, sucked cigarettes
fizzing as they lean into the edges of
shrilling corners, talk in nudges
and taunts, three ten-year-olds, too tough
for girls, though girls they'll brag of, soon enough,
their long, pale hair brokenly raked
beyond the line of last year's makeshift
barbering, frayed shirtcuffs falling short to
flash expensive watches, newly bought.

The city's greased and rapid
machinery is their passion; they'll work it
to the last cog, discovering all the loopholes—
how to tilt the pin-tables
and not lose the game, when to slip
their pocketful and saunter from the shop.
School can't detain them; they've cut the nets
of that soft playground. The lesson drifts
above their empty desks like a will read
solemnly to the disinherited.

Westminster Bridge veers up. They clatter down,
jump for its back, are straggling shadows, blown
and tiny as they run to see themselves
V-signing back from windows of black waves.
Further and further now from from the controls,
they wander out of history, though its spires
rise in gold above them. The clock's proud face
makes no comment, shines on some other place.

RULES FOR BEGINNERS

They said: 'Honour thy father and thy mother.
Don't spend every evening at the Disco.
Listen to your teachers, take an O level
or two. Of course, one day you'll have children.
We've tried our best to make everything nice.
Now it's up to you to be an adult!'

She went to all the 'X' films like an adult.
Sometimes she hung around the Mecca Disco.
Most of the boys she met were dead O level,
smoking and swearing, really great big children.
She had a lot of hassle with her mother;
it was always her clothes or her friends that weren't nice.

At school some of the teachers were quite nice,
but most of them thought they were minding children.
'Now Susan,' they would say, 'You're nearly adult—
behave like one!' The snobs taking O level
never had fun, never went to the Disco;
they did their homework during *Listen with Mother.*

She said: 'I'd hate to end up like my mother,
but there's this lovely bloke down at the Disco
who makes me feel a lot more like an adult.'
He murmured—'When I look at you, it's nice
all over! Can't you cut that old O level
scene? Christ, I could give you twenty children!'

He had to marry her. There were three children—
all girls. Sometimes she took them to her mother
to get a break. She tried to keep them nice.

It was dull all day with kids, the only adult.
She wished they'd told you that, instead of O level.
Sometimes she dragged her husband to the Disco.

She got a part-time job at the Disco,
behind the bar; a neighbour had the children.
Now she knew all about being an adult
and honestly it wasn't very nice.
Her husband grumbled—'Where's the dinner, mother?'
'I'm going down the night-school for an O level,

I am,' said mother. 'Have fun at the Disco,
kids! When you're an adult, life's all O level.
Stay clear of children, keep your figures nice!'

UNPLAYED MUSIC

We stand apart in the crowd that slaps its filled glasses
on the green piano, quivering her shut heart.
The cavern, hung with bottles, winks and sways
like a little ship, smuggling its soul through darkness.
There is an arm flung jokily round my shoulders,
and clouds of words and smoke thicken between us.
I watch you watching me. All else is blindness.

Outside the long street glimmers pearl.
Our revellers' heat steams into the cold
as fresh snow, crisping and slithering
underfoot, witches us back to childhood.
Oh night of ice and Schnapps, moonshine and stars,
how lightly two of us have fallen in step
behind the crowd! The shadowy white landscape
gathers our few words into its secret.

All night in the small grey room
I'm listening for you, for the new music
waiting only to be played; all night I hear nothing
but wind over the snow, my own heart beating.

THE STRAWBERRY MARK

(for Dave)

Every Sunday we'd set out at noon
and wear down the light to a dust of stars

before turning home. Our child went with us,
billowing the green sail of my smock.

Do you remember that farmer who disturbed
us on the shady edge of his corn? We ran like fire.

Monday would put us in our different places.
You worked. I queued, dragging the heavy basket.

The strawberries plumped as their price went down.
I ate them, craving you only.

Our walks got colder and shorter.
The house re-introduced us, two strangers.

Come November, I would find
the hem of the green smock suddenly drenched dark.

Alone, I walked and walked the edge of the world,
my breath the great wind there. You thought me lost.

Someone said: 'It's a girl!' You lifted the shawl
and saw the dappled scarlet on her thigh.

Twelve summers and many strawberries
later, the mark has gone,

the peculiar heat and fragrance of that summer
sealed, perhaps, in her smile. Or simply faded.

LATE GIFTS

They meet in the mornings over coffee,
their only bond work, and being married
to other people. They begin with jokes—
the chairman, the weather, the awful journey—
delicately pacing out their common ground.

Later, they expand into description.
Families, who might not recognise themselves,
are called up in brisk bulletins
edited for maximum entertainment.
(Gossip ignores their middle-aged laughter.)

She shows him a photo of her sons
tanned and smiling over fishing nets
one green June day, when her eye was steady.
He talks about his daughters, both away
at college. They admire everything.

Through the months more curious, more honest,
they cultivate small permissions, remember
each other in the fading summer evenings,
and suddenly get up from their lives
to hunt for a book or pick some fruit.

No quarrels cloud the gentle light between them.
They imagine how their adequate weekends
might shimmer with this other happiness,
and how, perhaps, they'd still end up with less
than haunts a gift of pears, a borrowed book.

A LATIN PRIMER

(for Kelsey)

Today, a new slave,
you must fetch and carry, obeying
plump nouns, obstreperous verbs
whose endings vacillate
like the moods of tyrants.
Say nothing. Do as you're told.
Dominus servum regnat.

Tomorrow, a legionary,
they'll have you building roads.
Clause by clause you'll sweat
to span counties, withstand armies
Pack the stones tight and straight.
Don't stop to pick flowers.
Milites progressi urbum ceperunt.

One day, you may discover
that even Rome was young.
And this is literature—
to hear your own heart-beat echo
in the bright streets of grammar
where poets lark and sigh,
and girls, like you, are choosy—
Da mi basia mille, deinde centum,
dem mille altera, dein secunda centum . . .

THE SKIN POLITIC

Sails for the dark blue trade routes
Guns for the jungle
Mulberry trees for Brick Lane
White skins for England.

Smiles for a passport
Pavements for wet walking
Ramadan for emptiness
White skins for England.

Airmail for memories
Shudders for dark nights
Swastikas for bus shelters
White skins for England.

Long words for governments
Short words for street corners
Last rites for promises
White skins for England.

A MARRIAGE

Mondays, he trails burr-like fragments
of the weekend to London—
a bag of soft, yellow apples from his trees—
a sense of being loved and laundered.

He shows me a picture of marriage
as a small civilisation,
its parks, rosewood and broadloom;
its religion, the love of children

whose anger it survived
long ago, and who now return like lambs,
disarmed, adoring.
His wife sits by the window,

one hand planting tapestry daisies.
She smiles as he offers her the perfect apple.
On its polished, scented skin
falls a Renaissance gilding.

These two have kept their places,
trusting the old rules
of decorous counterpoint.
Now their lives are rich with echoes.

Tomorrow, she'll carry a boxful
of apples to school. Her six-year-olds
will weigh, then eat them, thrilling
to a flavour sharp as tears.

I listen while he tells me about her sewing,
as if I were the square of dull cloth
and his voice the leaping needle
chasing its tail in a dazzle of wonderment.

He places an apple in my hand;
then, for a moment, I must become his child.
To look at him as a woman
would turn me cold with shame.

FLOATING GARDENS

Dusk drifts down in speckles, a dull sootfall
sticking to each clean edge and blade.
Am I asleep awake? The marigolds
light sudden waxy lamps that flicker out
in moments, leaving me futureless,
and the mind's secrets open, clear as stars.
They show me another garden where the warm
breath of the dying grass you whirled like grain
and scattered, moving patient as the sun
along each brightening strip, scents the air
and makes your absence almost tangible.
Do flowers fear the dark,
and shiver for the hands that tended them,
busy now with dinners, conversation?
Rooms are real, glowing through their glass
where families root and bloom, solid as brickwork.
But the gardens are lost to this world.
They whisper. They know it is not easy
to be sure of what we are or whom we love.

DECEMBER WALK

(i.m. W.A. Lumley)

1

Late winter noon,
the sky blue-black as taxis,
the street below
brimmed with fluorescence.
Typewriters stutter madly
as if they kept trying
somehow to re-shape the words
for bread or anger.
My father stands
in the narrow doorway
where a dim room meets
a darker hall.
His bent hands dangle,
useless even to smoke
a farewell cigarette.
He has only the threadbare
decision he stands up in,
and when they come for him,
no straitjackets or calming
drugs will be required.
Easy as a child,
he'll tiptoe with the strangers
to their white car.
Fled into this city,
this cradling honeycomb
where all the girls shine
and shirt-cuffs are clean,

I know that I have simply
followed him here,
that this could have been his chair.
He stands at my side,
rubbing the cold from his hands,
amused by his child's
new game—the full in-tray,
the memos, the poems—
and saying with his smile:
no hurry, no hurry.
We all have to go home.

2

Pacing behind him,
I imagine how light he must be.
The bearers' tall, black shoulders
would never admit it.
They are braced for immensity.
The organ takes up the pretence,
and the chrysanthemums, quaking
their frilly gold baroque
through icy chapel air.
In plain pews built
too narrow for kneeling
we remove our gloves
and pray from small books.
He was somebody once,
but sickened, and lost
the weight of himself.
He forgot our names
and wandered for years,
words melting off his back

like snowflakes. Now
as the altar screen slides
tactfully across
to blot out doomed wood,
I recall only a mood,
a flickering of smiled
irony, betraying
that willingness, flat and English
as the whited winter sky,
to be always disappointed
He was an unbeliever
in everything he did,
yet would have had a hand
in this, perhaps, approving
our boredom, the sad weather
and what there is of ash.

SMALL VIEWS

When a road ends in sky,
you know that the sea is breathing somewhere near;
that the land has admitted defeat,
signing its name regretfully, gracefully
in a scrawl of white hotels.

What happens now?
A string or two of lights, a timid pier,
damp huts to brew tea in;
a lack of view. Is this what matters most?
Is that why we're lured here?

We become child-minded
whenever we stare across water.
We cannot really believe
in a far coast rising to mirror ours.
So too we interpret the sky

whose clear gaze says we're its only world,
and if there are stars beyond the stars
they must be demons.
Down here on our tiny maps
we have heard no news of America;

no film-packed satellites
have retrieved the mist-wept fall of our horizon
How could we live without this prejudice?
How set sail without forgetting
that, sea by sea, we're merely travellers home?

THE FREEDOM WON BY WAR FOR WOMEN

From hassock, cradle-side and streaming walls—
The fogs of faith and wash-day—thin lives beaten
Blank and hung to weep, the fair are gone.
Raw-fingered saints who've tipped their pedestals

And dried their hands at Father Empire's yell,
They chivvy cautious husbands, rebel sons
With bloodiest white. But they'll take the same poison,
Hands deft among his axle-trees and shells.

True warriors, they were furnace-forged when bombs
Jumped roof-high. From tongue to lung the taste
Of lead rolled death. Massed engines pumped their Somme.

It was a flowering and a laying waste—
Man's skills found shining at the heart of woman,
His vengeance, too, expediently unlaced.

THREE POETS PLAY THE SAKÉ CUP GAME

Tying his proud syllables
to a scented branch,
the poet hears laughter.
He turns and sees the cup
lodged winking in some reeds.
It will never pass him now.
As life begins, the poet muses,
so it stops, without warning.
Haiku is the game in the middle.
'Have I won?' he asks. 'Or lost?'

2

The orange sake cup
throbs on the bright stream
with petals, like a migraine.
It's only one word he wants,
one last, ripe cherry
brimming with the juice of his poem.
The cup weaves nearer. Demons
toss him a flashy adjective.
He sighs, and scribbles.
Sometimes he can't bear to be a poet.

3

The idea grows.
He must be careful, careful.
Never mind the jeering,
winter's a difficult season
and this could be its soul.
He mustn't let it slip by

as the sake cup slips by.
When he wakes from the poem,
it's dark, the cherry has dropped
many leaves, his friends have gone.

from **Star Whisper** (1983)

A COLD DAWN

This is the sky that drank its bitter greenness
straight from Gdansk Bay.

This is the sky of the world, its forehead smeared
with the sacrifice of industry

and fouled breath. This is the sky
that pushes into my room and takes a picture

of the moment of childish tears after a parting.
The first machinery creaks awake outside.

Ice at a thaw. Blind hammers
intent on their fathering.

Soon every brain will be working,
shuttling the slackened parts of an obsolete engine.

The Division of Reptiles slides
into the square, announcing its dialectic

to the shipbuilder, hurrying
with lowered eyes over the bridge.

Blood? No, he thinks, *tears*
of rust, or perhaps cold tea.

So the snowstorm of light goes on
filling up the day

and all the small 'no's' are said
and lost in the treacherous 'yes.'

THE NAME OF NAMES

Because we belonged to a place of crossed-out names,
whose letters toted guns like border guards,
and even the trees, deadbeat,
quaked again at the thought of changing hands:
because the searchlights swung white corridors
down all points of the compass, and the wire
lay wreathes of twisted crosses on the snow—
and because the snow had lost all track of you—
I stayed in the trashed house that was our home.
Now I feel as if I'll never leave again.

I can't think of the past, the crossed-out names,
the burning stars stitched to the east of the heart,
without distrusting everything I am,
but you could trust words written by the hand
that stroked so lightly back the twins of hair
falling across your frown, their peaceful aleph.
I can't think of the future's windswept map
where trains invent enormous distances
past cities atom-fed, white-hot all night,
past forests black and dense as grammar books,
and not loathe time's dead beat.
But if anonymously you should come back
one day, and learn how near the old place is—
no work-camps now, no dogs to leap and tear—
turn and approach softly whatever's there.
Look in the dark that might have been our home.
Among the words that fell from me like dreams
until a kind of liberation came,
you might find hidden, love, your name of names.

GEOGRAPHY LESSON

Here we have the sea of children; here
A tiny piece of Europe with dark hair.
She's crying. I am sitting next to her.

Thirty yellow suns blobbed on cheap paper,
Thirty skies blue as a Smith's Salt-wrapper
Are fading in the darkness of this weeper.

She's Czechoslovakia . And all the desks
Are shaking now. The classroom window cracks
And melts. I've caught her sobs like chicken-pox.

Czechoslovakia, though I've never seen
Your cities, I have somehow touched your skin.
You're all the hurt geography I own.

HEART SUFFERER

He stands in his kingdom of cloth, the long rolls
Heaped in a stifling rococo all around him
And smiles at the visitors' compliments. His eyes
Are calm, however. He is no emperor now,
Merely a guide. Business is a small thing
Compared to a Bach fugue or even a prelude,
Though balancing by day his lost currencies.

He speaks his adopted tongue with a fluent crafting
Except for a few cut vowels. But the poets he quotes
Are all Hungarian, all untranslated.
He is recomposing a suite of piano music,
Remembered across the noise of thirty years,
This businessman, who makes out an order so briskly:
Three metres of small-check gingham in muted green.

His customers tonight are an English couple.
The man beats him occasionally at chess.
The woman, he doesn't know. The cloth is a gift.
She presses it to her face, smelling the sweetness
Of an orange giving its gold to the treacherous north.
He waits upon her choice. He feels December
Creep from the walls, whisper up through his soles.

Here are satiny linings, cerulean
Glints from the rarest birds, the earliest summers.
Here are the stripes of crops, a snow of flowers,
And now the flattened cities, tanks, collapsed
Angles of aircraft; table-cloths once dappled
By Sabbath candles, ravelling up in flame;
Small bodies sewn into the colourless dresses.

He turns off the lights (no one else is allowed to,
He explains shyly, it's an old superstition)
And thinks of his tall sons, determined never
To wake the switches of his dying kingom.
He climbs the stairs slowly, examining
The coats of his visitors—brash young cloth,
Not lasting. *Dust to dust*, his heart reminds him.

With luck, he'll leave its music at the door
Of his favourite cellar bar. A dish of prawns
Is light, easily swallowed. He breaks the necks
Deftly, sucks the juice from each stalked head
And wonders at his sin, the sea-clean flavor.
At pavement level, London chains its gods
In light; he worships none, but wins each day
By his own kind of fasting and atonement,
Time become paper-thin as the map of prawn shells.

THE MOST DIFFICULT DOOR

There is an ageing mirror by the stairs
And, next to that, the most difficult of doors.
This is where we live, the home's true heart.
Its furnishings, heaped for some moonlight flit,
Are combs and hats and scarves in slip-knots, all
Embodying the female principle.

I sometimes think they must have swum like clouds,
My daughters, through those sea-blue altitudes
Of birth, where I was nothing but the dark
Muscle of time. I bear the water-mark
As proof, but that my flesh could be so filled
And concentrated, heart to heart with child—

It mystifies me now. I want to draw
One back, and this time feel a proper awe
For the tiny floater, thumb-sucking on its rope,
Slumbering in the roar of the mother-ship,
Or let my palm ride switchback on the billows
Kicked in my skin by silvery, unborn heels.

Instead, through thinnest glass I watch them drift
At leisure down their self-sufficient street;
Their territory might be the whole of time
Like that of lovers in some midnight game,
This house their port where indolently they sight
Far out at sea the changing play of light.

Sea restlessness! It haunts the oldest vessel—
A shanty murmuring under a torn sail
That no harbour is safe, nor should be safe.

Only deep waters lend full weight to life.
The maths of stars is learned by navigation,
And the home's sweetness by the salty ocean.

This glass could cut a vista down the years,
Gathering suburban satins and veneers
To a sleepy London bedroom. Hair, long-greyed,
Glows animal again. They're half afraid
To see themselves, so shiny, crimped and pressed—
My grandparents, doll-perfect, wedding-dressed.

And now its stare borrows an older face—
My own. The moon inimitably displays
Her sun-love. Through these veils we snatch from death
Our dusty matter, light its eyes with myth.
Nature wants Children. Children sometimes want
The moon, the cup, the shield, the monument.

We've watched the comb reap sparks from our live hair;
Now for the putting-on of mock despair
As timeless as these little pouts and twists—
A rite we go through as the cold glass mists.
We know the brightness in each painted eye
Must often be the brightness of goodbye.

My floating daughters, as I leave I'll see
How you will one day look as you leave me,
How touch draws back, malingering, though the breeze
Of night is tugging gently at our sleeves.
Be wary, but don't fear the darkening street.
I give you this, my opened map of flight.

A CASE OF DEPRIVATION

A shelf of books, a little meat—
How rich we felt, how deeply fed—
But these are not what children eat.

The registrar rose from his seat.
Confetti danced, and thus were wed—
A shelf of books, a little meat.

We sang, for songs are cheap and sweet,
The state dropped by with crusts of bread—
But these are not what children eat.

They came demanding *trick or treat?*
We shut our eyes, and served instead
a shelf of books, a little meat.

Then on our hearts the whole world beat,
And of our hopes the whole world said
But these are not what children eat.

Two shadows shiver on our street.
They have a roof, a fire, a bed,
A shelf of books, a little meat—
But these are not what children eat.

AN EASTER GARLAND

1

The flowers did not seem to unfurl from slow bulbs.
They were suddenly there,
shivering swimmers on the edge of a gala—
nude whites and yellows shocking the raw air.

They'd switched themselves on like streetlamps
waking at dawn, feeling wrong,
to blaze nervously all day at the chalky sky.
Are they masks, the frills on bruised babies?
I can't believe in them,
as I can't believe in the spruces and lawns and bricks
they publicise, the misted light of front lounges
twinned all the way down the road,
twinned like their occupants, little weather-house people
who hide inside and do not show their tears—
the moisture that drives one sadly to a doorway.

2

My father explained the workings of the weather-house
as if he seriously loved such things,
told me why Grandpa kept a blackening tress
of seaweed in the hall.
He was an expert on atmosphere,
having known a weight of dampness—
the fog in a sick brother's lungs
where he lost his childhood; later, the soft squalls
of marriage and the wordier silences.

In the atmosphere of the fire
that took him back to bone
and beyond bone, he smiled.
The cellophaned flowers outside
went a slower way, their sweat
dappling the linings of their glassy hoods.

3

My orphaned grass
is standing on tiptoe to look for you.
Your last gift to a work-shy daughter
was to play out and regather
the slow thread of your breath

behind the rattling blades,
crossing always to darker green,
till the lawn was a well-washed quilt
drying, the palest on the line,
and you rested over the handlebars
like a schoolboy, freewheeling
through your decades of green-scented, blue,
suburban English twilights.

4

In the lonely garden of the page,
something has happened to your silence.
The stone cloud has rolled off.
You make yourself known
as innocently abrupt
as the flared wings of the almond,
cherry, magnolia;
and I, though stupid with regret,
would not be far wrong
if I took you for the gardener.

LINES ON THE SHORTEST DAY

(to Josepli Brodsky)

> *Since this / Both the year's and the day's deep midnight is.*
> John Donne
> 'A Nocturnal Upon St Lucy's Day, Being the Shortest Day'

It's the year's midnight (I won't count how many
Since your last candle shivered out); now only
Dust has designs
On the lost She who aped attentiveness,
And clasped your hand, its clever helplessness,
To Poetry's reins.

So you ride out love's sighs, and history's,
Across the pyromaniac centuries
To these bright streets.
Hot-line and waveband mesh the stars above;
Down here, the snow grows sluttish at the shove
Of booted feet.

As for the fact it's Christmas, there's no doubt
In London; neon and tinsel spell it out
Wherever you're turning,
And though the sun was sepulchred all day
There's a warm flush in the four o'clock night-sky
Of money burning.

Recruited to our throng, with a lean smile
You press your nose to these alchemical
Gold-brimming panes,
And deftly lift from each department store
A pocketful of burnished metaphor
For tawdry stones.

Dear ghost, dissolving inkwards, reinstate
The mourning tongue, the negatives we hate;
          Show hollow plenty
Your whiplash lines whose very commas bite
Until the tears that smart like crimson, light
          Our frozen city—

A grammar for all those who move less freely
Than snow, before the wind, or darkness stealing
          Across the floor;
For hungry queues whose meat and bread are doubt,
Closing ranks as the angle from 'sold out'
          Grows more severe.

The law in armour stalks their public squares
And rust-thin words are hammered to new powers
          On anvils of dissent.
At home, and tight, we chant a milder verse
To 'Peace on earth' (from Harrods to St Paul's)
          Fine sentiment—

Though not conceded by the governing will.
The West stages its cold-war vaudeville.
          And it's as though
We'd purposefully forgotten being schooled
That here our rulers rarely shoot the ruled
          For saying no.

Between our market-place of wind-up stars
And the gross state with its new breed of tsars
What's there to choose
But this hair's breadth infinity where you speak
And utter your peculiar heart-break
Part fact, part ruse?

Verse is the courtship dance that rarely fires
A Lucy dead in conscience or desires,
Yet tyrants fear
That poets are the thin ice of their times,
Their stanzas, tiny casements where red crimes
Brazenly peer.

Be patron, then, on an indifferent day,
Of every tongue's reluctance to betray
Its love with silence.
Bless, if you've power, the art of negatives,
If not the zero temperature that gives
Words iciness.

THE HEBREW CLASS

Dark night of the year, the clinging ice
a blue pavement-Dresden,
smoking still, and in lands more deeply frozen,
the savage thaw of tanks:

but in the Hebrew class it is warm as childhood.
It is Cheder and Sunday School.
It is the golden honey of approval,
the slow, grainy tear saved for the bread

of a child newly broken
on the barbs of his Aleph-Bet,
to show him that knowledge is sweet—
and obedience, by the same token.

So we taste power and pleasing,
and the white wand of chalk lisps on the board,
milky as our first words.
We try to shine for our leader.

How almost perfectly human
this little circle of bright heads bowed before
the declaration of grammatical law.
Who could divide our nation

of study? Not even God.
We are blank pages hungry for the pen.
We are ploughed fields, soft and ripe for planting.
What music rises and falls as we softly read.

Oh smiling children, dangerously gifted ones,
take care that you learn to ask why,
for the room you are in is also history.
Consider your sweet compliance

in the light of that day when the book
is torn from your hand;
when, to answer correctly the teacher's command,
you must speak for this ice, this dark.

STAR WHISPER

(for Eugene Dubnov)

If you dare breathe out in Verkhoyansk
You'll get the sound of Life turning to frost
As if it were an untuned radio,
    A storm of dust.

It's what the stars confess when all is silence—
Not to the telescopes, but to the snow.
It hangs upon the trees like silver berries—
    Iced human dew.

Imagine how the throat gets thick with it,
How many *versts* there are until the spring,
How close the blood is, just behind the lips
    And tongue, to freezing.

Here, you could breathe a hundred times a minute,
And from the temperate air still fail to draw
Conclusions about whether you're alive—
    If so, what for.

MUSEUM

Pro bono publico,
bright wood, clear labels;
a tasteful history
of sand and fossils,

motto-bearing plates
and, along one wall,
like the Apocalypse,
'The Coal Coast' in oils.

Out on the concrete copy,
dogs are walked. The flat
water takes a slice
of sun from the smokeless sky.

The schools line up to go,
but the men in caps
linger shadowily
over toy-town mines, dolls' ships.

They get the place by heart
like the last day at the pit
or the drawer in the kitchen
where the strainer's kept.

MARCH, HAPPY VALLEY

Days that are finely stretched and luminous
as the paper of a Chinese lantern, keep
the birds up late and whispering across
the valley, where a massive wind feigns sleep.
All down the heath-side, dangerously close
as heart-beats to a foot that wades deep grass,
hang violets in the strangeness of their blue.
Luggageless, perennially new,
with ancient heads that they can only bend,
they have arrived more quietly than the dew
to feel the perfect cold of where they stand.

The country has a used, dishonest face,
a look of sour back-streets where trade has died
though half the windows still pretend with lace.
Spring, the sweet spring, is a refugee child
grown old before his time, a hope displaced.

CHERCHEZ L'AIL

London that night was held by golden ropes
   Fraying through the river's black.
The 'Queen of Spain' with all her costly lives
Sat tight, as we sat, formal in our hopes,
The bottle on its ice-bed leaning back.
We touched the cloth with bright, impatient knives.

Tides turn, the damaged love-boat drifts away;
   The marriage-teasers walk
The plank, and one in torment almost screams,
But smiles instead. I sniffed my hands next day
To light those flames that stroked our ice-chink talk,
To meet you on the garlic breath of dreams.

WRITING THE CITY

Rhymes, like two different hands joining,
are those slightly archaic correspondences
I look for when in trouble. It's so easy
to start panicking in cities.

All roads lead to each other, sharing slick
anecdotes of combustion. They sell
tin lollipops, barren islands
and the one-way look for city faces.

Things happen and unhappen; cars, like eyelids,
blink time away. I'm due for demolition . . .
Thar's why I stand so long in the Poetry Section,
and buy apples just to slice them into cradles.

SKINS

There are those that time will carelessly perfect:
Leather, wood and brick fall derelict
As if aware they charmed us as they slip;
This deal table, strung like a harp
With a silky glissando of dark grain
Blooms like a lover from the hands it's known.
Scrawlings of knife and bottle, child and guest
Have warmed its heart, a rough autumnal feast
Spilled into soil, becoming nutriment;
The wood's more deeply wood because of it.
But there are others, the most loved and rare,
Time told them once, of which the years despair.
Laughter has scribbled not itself but pain.
Each face is fallen on hard times of bone.
Money will court them first, and then deride them.
There are no masks but sorry stones to hide them.
Yet to the end they haunt disgusted mirrors,
As close as love, and steal with snow-lipped fingers
From little, lying, scented jars each night,
Skins that are pillow-shadows by first light.

LULLABY FOR A FIRST CHILD

This timid gift I nurse
as the one clear thing I can do.
I am new and history-less
as the name on your wrist, as you.
But flesh has scored a deep kindness
ready to welcome you.
Take it, a little silver
into your small purse.
There it will gather interest—
the warm, bright weight of you.

FROM *REGENT'S PARK CROSSINGS*

(for W.H.)

It will quite eclipse Napoleon.
THE PRINCE REGENT,
on seeing John Nash's plans for the Park

Love then and even later was the whole concern of everyone's life.
That is always the fate of leisured societies.
ATTR. TO NAPOLEON BONAPARTE

1 *Grand Designs*

A perfumed handkerchief,
a bedspread of silk, a park.
His sun-sleeked horse carries him,

the seaside Prince,
away from affairs of state
at a glorious, graceful cancer.

Taker of air and of slender hands,
he is the patron
of the three-hour lunch-hour.

In his memory, two glasses
kiss in a buried wine-bar.
He has left an art of dalliance,

its lovely formalities;
a path broad as four coaches,
a bank of encrimsoned silver,

drawn swords of fleur-de-lis,
ducks in fancy dress,
footmen and maids abandoned in the grass.

rubbished and outstripped
by nature's great law of green.

Now the sky glows the colour of lampshades
in a bistro, the trees are black,

crowding big-shouldered like waiters,
priests, aunts, pallbearers.

Our flustered, red-faced lovers
can't get beyond the *hors d'œuvres*. They dip their fingers,

while the chestnut-blossom ticks,
ticks with the sound of a pen-nib totting numbers.

5 *Mediocracy*

Nothing here is sad or complicated.
The Open Air Theatre will perform
the same three comedies again this year.

The dolphin boy is a legendary confection,
the drinking fountain, a folly.
The Bandmaster sticks to the light classics,

his shiny regiment buzzing around Sousa,
as if Schoenberg, after all,
had chosen a sensible trade.

Et in Arcadia ice cream
and billowing deckchairs.
Each grassy lap is nurtured by the state gardeners,

and picnicked on by the masses.
It's an English Utopian's dream
where the laws (against walking

on certain banks, and fishing
the duckponds) are so pointless,
everybody obeys them.

A quiet, shared happiness bathes
like a sunset, each limited choice,
and only the very few

are tortured by mediocrity.
They are, of course, free to leave
at once by the Golden Gates.

6 *Nothing*

Your absent presence spoke
softly across the summer
with your haunting absence.

I was between the two,
a child whose timid look,
swinging from eye to eye,

is a metronome of dread,
knows nothing, nothing, nothing
but his guilt-ridden innocence.

So shifts this sea of grass
beneath the wind, until
the sun burns it to stillness

and gold. But what is kept?
The daylight turns its back,
slips the transfigured quilt.

9 *To Construct a Rainbow*

Tulips, footsteps, history
unwind long ribbons through the forgetful green.

The trees rain petals – *da mi basia mille.*
The sky is playing at war.

The forces of darkness ride out.
But the sun, great pacifist,

turns a cloud-cheek, shows us
the long bruise of a promise.

I step into the boat;
it rocks on its packed fathoms.

God sends the rainbow love
springing from heart to heart

just once in a while; not for long
may the dull beasts float in such gladness.

10 *Phaedrus*

The souls of lovers, said Socrates
to his young companion,

can complete their wings only
by embracing Philosophy.

The way hard, these friends
paddled the stream, arousing

a bright complication of water.
Through the hot midday

their silvery dialectic
shimmered below plane-leaves.

Summer wings stirring the air,
love talked itself to oblivion.

They parted not with a kiss
but a prayer, honouring wisdom.

11 *Dark Path*

Beneath this unlucky white May tree,
we found all we could understand of love.

So we went deeper and deeper down the green path
whose stems grow thickly together like a great friendship,

as if we were dreamed by some old nature-god,
and bound and garlanded with children's hands.

Darker and steeper the green path plunges still,
but now I've lost you; it's late.

Gnats play like little lights above the ghost crowds
of Queen Anne's lace, the lake seems made of dead rain.

What if all that has happened which we named
desire cries suddenly to be renamed?

Here come my two black swans, desultory.
They snap their beaks in the water and complain.

One always in tow to the other, through the seasons
they float their listless epithalamium.

Better, they'd say, an unadoring pair
than one in deep love, alone.

12 *Numen Non In Est*

The city's ravishing makeup
is all over the sky
in teary streaks;

the sky is hurrying out.
The frightened flowers have sunk
their last coins into moonlight.

A runner heralds himself
with the gasps of crushed leaves.
The breath he unstintingly pours

is kept by the wraith trees;
now they're as lost as he is.
In the clearings are temples,

their pitch roofs low
as frowns. They are dedicated
only to shade.

All winter they'll stand empty
for the dark god has escaped;
his love is everywhere.

13 *The Rain and Time*

It was the rain, not time,
that drove us from our seat:
rain's fresh, abrupt and sweet

hilaritas, teasing us
with the bookish smell of dust,
the brightened traffic swishing

beyond that iron goodbye—
the gate—which suddenly
had become impassable.

We rushed from tree to tree,
caught not in time but the rain.
All night it stroked the dark,

and this was happiness—
not to care whom you held
while the flickering, whispering threads

held us. And somewhere still
on these dry, forgettable days,
perhaps it is stitched for us

dancingly, in minutes,
our life between-lives as it runs
caught both in time and the rain.

14 *Fallen*

The sky is leaning and leaning
towards the park, grey breast
suffusing the green with shadow.

The light is crushed between them.
They exchange slow breaths
in heart-to-heart dumbness.

I touch, deep in my pocket,
horse-chestnuts found for the children
and never given.

Dressed in their creamy caps,
they glistened like brushed colts,
silkenly sat in the grass—

creatures of the dew
and a moment's lending;
impossible, but I took them.

Now there's no need to look.
I can feel how the light has gone,
how the tree is dead in them.

They are museum pieces—
old conscience money, carved men
for a game of imagining.

15 *Appearances*

How like a branch a man
who stands in a high tree.

Blackly he bends on the bending
bough in the blind light.

Smoke rising towards him,
he patiently saws, diminishing

his own margin of safety,
He'd fall with his branch, of course,

in the next frame of the comic,
pursuing to its limit

this art of camouflage
now gathering its echoes—

a moorhen's weed-green legs—
the absurdly familiar smiles

of two who have just met
and share by chance their seat.

16 *Clouds*

The park flattens.
its perspectives simplify

to a statement of loss.
The flower-lights in their casements,

the lattices, the dark dells
have been drawn upwards, kept

by fat-lipped angels.
Mere blanks remain, an earth

too dumb for questioning whether
life or death enthrals it.

We all wear coats now—
gardeners, bulbs, the sky.

Forgetful snow will fall soon,
blue shadows thicken upon

the burial place, the closed book;
a story told for one.

from **Direct Dialing** (1991)

A PRAGUE DUSK, AUGUST 21ST 1983

About a subjugated plain,
Among its desperate and slain,
The Ogre stalks with hands on hips,
While drivel gushes from his lips.
W.H. Auden

1

When his broad shoulders turn
in their leaf-coloured uniform
and square up to a doorway
on Revolucni Street,
he might be any soldier
and the bar, any girl,
its response no more than a certain
heightened inattention.
He orders beer and seems
as innocent as his thirst,
straining his young white throat
to greet the last drop,
but the pearl of Mitteleuropa
has dimmed behind him;
shadows slide unchecked
from the medallioned buildings
scaffolded up to the waist,
numb veterans who have learned
how short the life of honour.

He smiles, provincial, brash,
half-tame. The careful hands
that have served his purposes
slink off and busy themselves
with rows of glasses, small

change. Eyes follow him out,
each glint of hate a coin
with its own private value.

2

That he could not master speech
no longer seems important.
Perhaps only a poet
word-trafficking in the free
market economy
of Oxford or New York
would have thought it a fatal weakness.
One blast of his breath was enough
to seal the twelve bridges.
With a few phrasebook phrases
he is armed for years to surprise
and amuse the populace,
his weight sunk in its silence.
Impassioned flattery
on the cut of his Westerner jeans
is not expected when,
naked as his fists,
he strides down Vaclavski Namesti
with his shuffling train of echoes:
what happens, happens without us.
We forget only the present.
It is the glue of memory
that hardens round the nerves
of the empty August city.

3

Going home on the metro
the children chatter
but the mother is almost asleep.
Some sweet, unscripted dream
wanders across her face,
follows the droop of her arm
to the grasses that nod in her lap.
It's already dark
on the staircase where she hushes
and stumbles; light from outside
shines on the two pairs of shoes
placed at each nuptial doorway,
intimate and exhausted,
moored like little boats
in an ocean of drudgery.
When she too, at last,
is sitting in stockinged feet
and the children asleep,
she will recall each detail
of the picnic: how the country
they walked through never changed,
monotonous and tender
as the afternoons of motherhood;
how tall the grass became
when they lay down to rest
and the stalks rose silvery miles
and whispered to the sky.

A SOVIET ARMY TENOR

The Russian voice, it's said
has risen a whole tone since the nineteen-hundreds,

pushed up by nervous insincerities,
but the song that flickers high off the cassette

was earthed before the censor's chalk screamed
on the clean slate, or irony bit its lip.

And the choir, gathering leisurely reinforcements,
is only a windswept platoon of firs,

a chained sigh, an unhonoured
show of strength in the field of robbed time.

Medals burn in the studio-lights. But listen
to the soft, irregular, excited breathing

of the only animal said to have a soul.
He can silence his own kind

in multiples, blindly obeying his hands,
yet, when the mood takes him,

he remembers his disproven soul, and wishes
that every army could become a choir,

and the battleships dip their turrets
in shame at having borne the names of men.

OUTSIDE OSWIECIM

1

Let me tell you the story of days, handsomely printed
in dawn and darkness, in sleep
and in burnt-eyed longing for sleep.

2

It puzzles the secular light, this polyphony
of dim cries. I wasn't there, I heard nothing,
but the air fills, and forces breath to sing them.

3

When the train banged to a stop and whispered 'where?',
then they began. Some rose, some fell. *The sky*
rushed in like sea, we opened our mouths, it drank us.

4

The hardest hope to lose is the last and smallest.
Those words on the gate, some dreamed of them, and loved
to walk in their shade, suck out the iron of their promise.

5

In the night, the light; in the light, the wire;
in the wire, the heart; in the heart, the world;
in the world, Oswiecim.

6

Dumb narrative curiosity keeps you from the wire
how many times?You watch yourself, amazed,
whipped to a panting run past outstretched arms.

7

It was Erev Shabbat, evil was fallible.
A shaved girl smiled in the sun. An angel had murmured
'Amen' before he saw the gesturing dead.

8

And what if his lord had heard that some of them
were raging animals, and still sent daybreak, still
sent no one to stroke them with their names?

9

No, no, the question is obsolete.
Nothing sees nothing. Mercy was up to us.
Our mouths bit down on nothing.

10

Emblem, exhibit, witness—Husserl's suitcase
flanked the rust-brown pile. The cold twine of its handle
I touch, then grasp for a faceless, weightless stanza.

11

Child, enchanted at gun-point, whose child are you?
Come here, take off your cap, don't cry.
How is it possible I can make no difference?

12

Oh they crowd in, death's kindergarten. Small grazes
scared them once. Their eyes are always yours.
I'd take their pain, here, where your absence is.

13

I loved in you, yes, what made you strangest.
The desert gave you its shadows. I'd watch for ever
the poise of your smile, its mocking tenderness.

14

Another race is only an other, strolling
on the far side of our skin, badged with his weather.
In love or hate we cast looks, hooks; get it wrong.

15

How shall I bear your indifference without hate?
It stirs in the dust, a length of hose. If I burn
how shall I not flex my whip near your eyes?

16

No, come away, bury yourself in the pit
of tears, be ash and stone, your stare
like his, a star.

17

They beckoned, they turned their limbs this way and that,
they whispered, you tried to get near enough to hear,
bur the heat roared at you—*take your eyes, run.*

18

Not 'the six million', not 'the holocaust',
not words that mass-produce, but names. One name;
Husserl's, perhaps. His favourite food, his new watch.

19

Chosen to illustrate the Shibboleth's Tale;
An illumination from the Book of Fire,
Sand and Next Year; chosen to be most mortal,

Our pyramid swam and sank through the nitrogen
Fog as starving crystals ate our air.
Christ, to whom the soldier said 'Go on,
Call down your god if he's got ears and brains'
You would have understood our short-breathed terror.
Poor rebel son, you shared our tribal chains
That day, but now we wipe you from our mirror.

So we died for the last unforgeable scrap—
Our land. Got free for being something harder
Than walking zoo-meat. Fought like the Crusader
To nail our resurrection to the map.

NORTHERN WOODS

Small enterprises line the exit roads
out of London . . . then the bankruptcies . . .
and the long haunting of her absence begins
in a delirium whitened by birch trees.
They sidle past, existentialist poseurs,
with a soft slippery shine that is barely a shine –
what light is there in the world for them to borrow?
Go on, they say, dissolve into drugs and tears;
we are her trees, we are your memories
blank with all she could not bear to tell you.
But I never cry. I just keep driving, staring.
When I left her for the last time, our hopes
the sea-smashed continent, my flight-bag heavy
as a new tongue, I learned to swallow fire.
Now the colourless bottle leaves me sober
as a vision of birch woods, growing colder
and cloudier as they get to Pietarsaari.

BLOCKADE

Europe has been broken:
a panacea of banks,
steel cladding, the black
fugue of Berlin.

Oh Linden Tree, oh Linden
I cannot breathe
without your small hands, your great shade.

AUBADE

Light as a rose
he sleeps beside
his first cradle,

intent on stillness
but breathing firmly
as if breath would always

give itself back.
He has travelled far
to be in his flesh,

to learn what happens
and to forget.
His existential

smile is perfect.
It tells me how
he will offer himself

when the time comes.
But for now he will keep
his excellent secrets—

the glossy function
of heart and lungs,
arms and legs,

the legend of his mouth.
His voice sleeps,
his sex sleeps.

In the faint shine of
morning when
flesh can be chilled,

I draw up the sheet
and cover him
to save us both.

VOCATION

Is it poetry I'm after at those moments when
I must clothe your hands in mine or comfort your shoulders—
so bare and neglected sometimes when we wake—
or press your mouth to taste its uncurling flower?
Is that which seems so fleshly and truthful merely
a twisted track into words, a way to leave you
for your image? Art is tempting, a colourful
infidelity with the self, and doubly feigning
when what is repossessed secretly by one
was made by two. And I wish I could pour a poetry-vodka
into twin glasses we'd gulp unanimously
('I poison myself for your health' the appropriate toast)
but only a poet would have acquired the taste
for such a strange distillation; you'd never warm
to heavy-petting dactyls, the squeak and creak
from locked, suburban stanzas. And so my fingers,
dancing alone, are less than content. They perceive
how they have clung to moral adolescence.
Their vocation now could be simply to talk to your skin,
to take you at kissing-time; later, to close your eyes
by stroking the lashes lightly over cheekbones
flushed with some high, bright, childish fever, and so
write the poem in the touch-shapes of darkness
and let it end there . . . They are on the tip of trusting
this silent, greyish room, its astonishing view
fading from metaphor to the life with you.

IN THE CLOUD OF UNKNOWING

Goodbye, bright creature.
I would have had you
somewhere on solid earth,
wings clipped to pale

shoulder-blades,
and your fleecy head
a chrysanthemum, darkly
grown from my pillow.

I would have kept my tongue
for what salt weepings
it could tease from your finest
silences.

But it was written
into your book of life
that I should be brief.
Forbidden to count

the ways, denied
et cetera,
I worshipped the stone
from your supper-time plum,

the little hairs gleaned
in tears from the sheet.
Metaphysical desire
was all they would bear,

a bandage of art
for the low sob
of the vernacular,
a condition of prayer.

Now when I wake
and the dawn light names
your perfect absence,
I am at home,

lapped again
in my earliest language,
the vocatives tense
with desire and distance:

'Thou who art called
the Paraclete';
'After this our exile';
'Oh Sacred Heart!'

Dear iconoclast
forgive these texts
their cloudy haloes.
The intent pen burns

its slow path through
the slant rain of Greek,
the stars of Hebrew
. . . to touch your hem?

No, it was never
possible.
The old mystics knew
as they closed the book

on the dancing colours,
worn out with words
never made flesh
and with flesh that fought

their long abstraction.
They listened a moment;
the breath-soft footstep
in the cloisters faded

as always to sighs;
the cold congress of leaves
in darkening autumn;
the wind's dissolution.

PAVANE FOR THE LOST CHILDREN

When you rest in my arms and your heart
quietens against mine
I think of a midnight kitchen,
the kettle muttering on the lowest gas,
and the baby forgetting to feed,
lips plumped like a little mollusc
that is almost losing its grip.
They could not relinquish survival,
those lips; I knew what they dreamed of
would keep arousing them
to fits of greedy, absent-minded tugging.
So I sat on, enthralled
by thirst, by plenitude.

This, too, is our grown-up devotion
when fatigue is most pressing:
to pretend we will never put each other down
and drift singly away on
sleep's disappointing persuasions;
such lowly forms of life, so deeply marine,
we cannot move apart, or know what time is,
but are turned like bivalves on the lifting wave
that has promised us to the sand.

TIME TROUBLE

I know all about these German wristwatches.
They try to wake you with tinny, insect-like tunes
as the digits flip over on your bedside table
and my old-fashioned minute hand
flies to your neck and whispers nervously
with that little pad of fat where your head is thrown back
because you're still in an ecstasy of sleep,
and your suitcase not yet packed.

Once upon a time
they'd take me to admire the German clock
in the museum. There were wooden figures inside it:
Jesus at wooden supper
with his twelve wooden apostles.
And when it struck three, they said,
the apostles filed out
and all bowed woodenly to Jesus
except Judas, who swung round the wrong way.

I never stayed to see this remarkable dumbshow.
By a minute to three, I was going to be sick;
I turned my back on the clock, the crowd
fell apart with a hiss.
As I race down the shadowless aisles,
though the horrible whirring has not yet begun,
I can see it all perfectly—
mad Jesus, his nodding guests,
and Judas, the simple materialist,
turning on his clockwork,
showing us his chalk-white face.

WINTER

It begins in secret
with mist, a dazed bee
in the lavender-bushes
and radiators mild
as human skin.
This would be May
to your serious habitat,
the iron-black river
that is its heart line,
wobbly as a frontier,
untrammelling itself
in endless dissatisfaction.
I think of the Burlaki
trussed in rope
like performing bears,
who trudged the plashing weight
of their servitude
to the rhythm of the thaw.
You bow your head,
fists on the table,
chest-notes swelling,
and silence the room
with their empire of grievance.
In your perilous climate
the wind has already fastened
stiff white graveclothes
on the auburn water.
It settles everything
like the hand of a lover.
So the winter river
accepts its birthright

calmly, as you must –
the massive silences,
the gift of utter cold—
locked in its own
solid crystal, surveyed
by a few tethered craft
hungry for a new trade
of skins and revolution.

ESCAPE FROM WHITE

Here, people's eyes, like the cities of this country
Are large and clear; never does the soul's tumult
Move the pupil with an exrtraordinary glance;
Never does desolation cloud them over long.
ADAM MICKIEWICZ,
'Forefathers' Eve'

Slowly, the bruise of afternoon lavender
deepens to bilberry, and slowly it seems to withdraw
from my approach, the sea-coloured coastline of sleep.
An edge of chalky moon appears, gets cloud-lost;
the book in my hand thins to another window.
Where in this walled city shall I go, where shall
I turn in the almost-white June night, and evade my need of you?

The cathedral swims like a whisper out of the sweat
of coppery lights. What nerve it takes to retrace
our descent into heavenly ordinariness when we roamed,
camera-hung tourists, hand-in-hand through St Stephen's
on a midsummer morning quiet as ourselves;
when, moved by your extraordinary glances,
I saw you admire the parochial, upright, lawn-trimming,
France-hating, surly soul of this dreariest county.

I was busy observing you with my old affection
for the edges of maps, that breath of the East you bring,
irresistible as the anecdotes once told me
by the milliner's girl, my Kentish grandmother,
whose hair as she swanned by the Medway glistened so black
the sailors sang at her 'Japalady!' If only
you'd naturalise me to your strangeness, I too might gaze
on this cabbage patch with tender, sea-grey eyes.

Idiomatic now, you perfect your tongue
with irony and bad grammar. Who would guess
from your study of gardens, supermarkets, cars
and American-English, that your true pursuit
is a moral example; how, in secret anguish,
you whisper to the child that dares not hear you
'But look how well this other one tries to behave!
Why can't you do the same?' And you almost pray
for the end of that damaged life, abandoned now
to the crocodile technicians of survival.

Each day abroad takes you curiously closer
to the narrow, silent, intimate hospital-bed
where the flesh is kept alive but whitely blank,
and you stare into eyes that cannot sleep or see,
their last wild doubt fixed in a glaze of sedation,
until the lavender dusk, the cathedral and my hands
with their foolish island behaviour of grasping and closing,
fade into the sombre night of your pilgrimage.

From the moment of touchdown you were free to fly,
and, at the first embrace of an *inostrantsa*,
to enter the terrible candour of homesickness.
Sometimes its waves swell to such a height,
I fear for your life; sometimes I think your heart breaks
whenever I say your name. If love exists,
is there more love in it than truth in *pravda*?
What can it do but take from you this gift
of night and bear the mourning it permits?

A JEWISH CEMETERY

1

At dawn they are one great shadow, whispering.
They are warning their children:
don't break the backs of your books.
Sunset. The shadow multiplies;
the backs break.

2

Among the swaying sighs
and the candlestubs, gothic with catarrh,
wanders the upright citizen. He is bored
and uneasy. He shoves the broken bits
of alphabet with his illiterate boot.
What else, these days, can you do with the past?

3

The closed books.
East looks West and sees East.
West looks East and sees West.
The apocalypse rides both ways.

4

Names must often be silences
in this city, in this world.
His block of flats is dark
and hollow like a chimney.
I climb it twice a day,
doubling my heartbeat
as I touch the bell that bears
his faded, biblical name.

My hope spirals up
and falls back, levelling
with my lack of hope,
a conversation of kinds
between the flame and the ash,
between the name and its silence
in this city, in this world.

GREETINGS FROM DÜSSELDORF

A cobbled yard, an impatient bronze colt
fenced in by spears, a livid spire or two;
I've learnt to pick these charming fragments out
from the money-boxes thick in every crater,
and make up a camera-fib, a street in filter,
that saw the Emperor once, or a hurrying Jew.

Admiring a sleek old fräulein's haute couture
(if you must be old, be tall, I always say)
Over a mineral water in Königsallee,
I woo the big names like an editor:
Schumann stumbles outside the head office
of Mannesmann (the looped double-M's
a gas-blue cross-stitch fallen from the stars)
and claws cadenzas in the laundered grass:
Heine on Bolkerstrasse slowly climbs
to his mattress grave above the Schwinken Grill,
praising God he's lost his sense of smell—
but these are my ghosts, not the bürgermeister's.
The roads are young, the young wear pink or white
with their tans. Midnight's rush-hour, every door
a jumping rainbow. You, in love, post-war,
would rate this city of stylish appetite.

DIRECT DIALLING

To trade in bliss
alone would never
be permitted us;
I understood this
from the start, although,
girlish enough,
I bought the dress,
and fed the scene
to my moment-adoring
Polaroid;
a little window
of flower-dotted green
that trembled in
your attentive hand.

But our faces, sad,
already told us
of time and the state—
their thirsty methods:
the prisoner reading,
heart-in-mouth
a thumb-stained letter
three winters old;
his wife bringing
his yearly half-hour,
like a wound they must both
stroke to bleeding.
Our kindlier pain
is simply this
rinsed teapot packed
in a cardboard box
with your cook's knives.

Where the law can't reach
mischance has set
his ancient looms;
he doesn't forget.

We faced across
the empty table;
could no more touch
than if watched. You,
silently smoking,

re-read the airmail,
its soldierly lines
of refusal shaky,
barbed like wire.
'What can I say
to your invitation?
Do you suggest
I betray my country?'
Then, later on,
'All my friends are dying.
I'm old and alone.'

Letters, phone-calls—
those vanishing sparks
in the great places
of absence and
fidelity;
the summer nights
ringed by ice.
Prometheus,
you wake each day

in your distant city,
stung in the ribs
by the acid spear
of prison-food;
and when you sleep
it's a kind of flight,
desperate, intense,
and, you say, dreamless.

We stand in line
to snatch a moment.
Our conversations,
furtive, hoarse,
hang by a thread
at midnight. Where
could we build our house,
by what dispensation
secure the loose sands,
the iron winds—
and our sturdy, late,
bilingual child
scatter, regather
the brightened stones
of all your loves?

SIXTEEN DANCERS

1

One night in our first week of marriage
you asked me to meet you in your favourite square.
It's easy, you said. I was to look for the postcard
you'd sent me once in Prague.
I remembered the small, feminine fountains,
how I had stared into their silvery weather
and tried to taste the sea.
Now my feet crunched pigeon-food, gravel, wet ice.
And there was the lion you'd climbed, jeans slithering
on the cold bronze, ten years ago, to shout
for Ho Chi Minh. You were late. Traffic snarled
in circles; I waited at the centre.
How small it was, after all, this famous square.
I looked down at my coat, my shoes, my handbag.
Gifts. Yours. London's. Not mine.
And then that English snow I'd refused to believe in
came feathering into the wind, little iron tongues
licking my face. My shoulders had turned to salt
as I stared east, towards home.

2

The tournament hall was like school,
with tables, and a ticklish, whispering silence.
I wasn't scared, I always did well at school.
I decided not to look at my opponent.
He was bigger than me, and we both knew he'd lose.
Parents, opponents, boyfriends, the state—
I laughed at all of them, I was never scared.
My mother dragged my hair back, plaiting it

cruelly, tugging my brains into three.
I snipped the plait off whole,
and pegged it on the kitchen line; she screamed.
I revelled in such private enterprise,
the thrust of Machiavellian knights and cut-throat
bishops; power flickering like black magic
from palace to proletariat and back.
It was a picture-book I'd never tire of,
and each new story always began the same:
once upon a time there were two great kings.
One lived in the east, and one the west.
And they were enemies though they were brothers.
Each knew the other king like his own face.

3

Some heads had been guillotined from the family album.
No one seemed to know why.
Poor faceless ones, I searched for evidence
of wickedness in watch-chains
or the grey folds of skirts where wrists lay broken.
At last their wounded innocence burned through,
silencing my childish accusations,
like the starry cherry-flowers on Namesti Miru.
They murmured: The Russians are here!
I was fifteen. It was thrilling, like the first taste
of melon each year, or plunging into the water
at Marienbad. The walls burst into posters,
the wind chased leaflets, hands flew everywhere.
The soldiers lounged and smiled like elder brothers.
Then the holiday was over,
the grown-ups silent as suitcases.
Our leader bowed his head, got into the Chaika.

The chairs stood back, as one by one,
my friends, no longer thirsty, left the singing.
They were like the people in the photograph
changing colour as I lay the page
on wood first, then my hand.
I sulked. My mother cried. My face grew thin.
I moved my wooden men to win, to win.

4

When they teach you your past is a lie,
they extinguish your future.
When the party-machine drives words into your mouth,
starvation becomes acute.
When friends disappear, the door of your heart bursts
open merely to reveal another door.
When the spotless spring parade shines on the trees,
you blink, and brush the petals from your eyes.

5

You were the reigning British Champion,
your suit like a blue coffin, your hair like leaves.
Beneath the fire-weeping chandelier,
sat Timman, neatly torturing Polugayevsky.
The hall was emptying. I'd won my game.
Yours was adjourned. A small crowd had gathered
at the smell of blood.
We stood together, held our breath and watched.
In the silence I felt your concentration lapse.
You touched my arm, and we walked softly out,
linking smiles in a world of foregone conclusions.

6

You courted me smartly, eloquent, careerist,
but perfect-mannered, versatile at checkpoints,
customs, hotel-desks. Our sweet receptions
bloomed among the low-line teak veneer
like an elaborate, creamy, high rococo,
tumbled out of nowhere, out of time.
And this, like time, was always quite beyond us—
a liberty we took, and couldn't take,
the morning after, homing to our boards
and clocks, the slow, meticulous invasions;
nationality seeping back, the silver cups
spreading their wings, the draped flags, the speeches,
the return ticket, and the correct papers.

7

Architects, accountants, friends from Oxford,
arrived at eight in the flat you called the cupboard,
and I, the manor.
Your eyes challenged them with a lovely fire,
as if you'd risked your neck to bring me here.
(The builders had only just left,
taking the earthquakes and the thunder-storms
but leaving the rainbows, as you had commanded.)
The flat was floured and trembling like a geisha.
Your friends pushed everywhere,
coughing a little, spilling drinks, at home.
One, I remember, spoke Czech:
and I, on my third vodka, told the joke
with the ice-and-lemon punch-line: what are the Russian
troops doing in Prague? They are looking
for those who invited them.

8

Sticky Fingers, Soldier Blue, Rough Trade:
I walk, take taxis, walk. My carrier bags
multiply. It rains. The pavements darken,
the dust smells antique. My feet get wet.
I don't care, my shoes have turned to knives
in spite of hours of choice and wads of plastic.
I'm in the wrong element. As for marriage,
it cost me a country. Once, I queued
all day for a chrome teapot, dumb with hope.
I never dreamed of flight as now I dream—
in *samizdat*, my thoughts fluttering
always towards my murderer, my accomplice,
whose fingers check me, who looks up and smiles.

9

You know how it is with us.
Living out of suitcases, we fly
from game to game, from story to story,
new faces on the loose change in our pockets.
You know how lonely it is—
the faint taste of a different language,
and the hotels, always the same yet not quite,
and the smiles at the opening dinner, the same, but not . . .
and nothing ever quite real.
You know what it is to win,
and how the rules change then,
or how we think the rules change then.

10

Marriage as an inventory:
mine, the Bohemia crystal;
yours, the Chinese rug;

mine, the silver fox,
the dolls, the rosewood box
of marbles, the kitchenware, its brave colours.
Yours, most of the books,
and all but one of the war games.
Mine, the thirst;
yours the cup.
Mine, the fault;
yours, the freedom from guile.
Mine, the manor, ruined.
Yours, the cupboard, empty.

11

The radio, left till last
because we can't decide,
squats on the floor and mutters to itself.
We would orphan it if we could.
Instead, we try and listen to its news.
Someone should be making tea;
someone should be quietly crying.
But everywhere it talks about is far away.
There is no mention of our fallen city.

12

Postcards telling jokes or lies—
I could write home on any of them,
send them from nowhere, never to arrive.
The stones of Prague, the sharpness of your eyes
I shall never see clearly again.
Ten years on, what do I know about you?
That you have a wife. Her name.
That her star is Virgo and she is virtuous.

That she has fair hair and is fully armed.
And what do you know about me?
That my victories are few. That I defect
regularly from those dictatorships
my lovers make of passion. That I claim
more freedom than there is in any world,
except the world of men.
Still I'd go down your winter streets again
to break a glass for one last toast. Bright-lipped
with sweet liqueur, we'd kiss and drink to life—
the life no kisses ever made less bitter.

13

How impassively they face each other,
the fighting men, before the players arrive.
A woman in overalls hoovers round the tables
indulgently. The fighting men exchange
the wan smiles of platoons on Christmas morning,
remembering cigarettes and oranges,
and what they still have left of being human.
The woman slides her hoover
noisily into the passage.
Dust twinkles in a sun-shaft, breakfast smells
seep from the kitchens. It is quiet, domestic.
The fighting men seem to have chosen peace
before the players arrive.

14

One eye on the clock, one ear on silence,
we take our sixteen paths into the darkness.
Outside, the universe of moves is flowering.
We have some choice. It dwindles. Who or what

chooses how we chose need not be asked.
It is enough to see that acreage
shine at our feet: first, the unharvested
squares of sun and shade; later, what's left
in the democracy of broken hopes—
this we call freedom, I and my sixteen dancers.

from **The Greening of the Snow Beach** (1988)

RUSSIAN LESSONS

(including the theme music of *Dr Zhivago*)

1

This is a revolutionary song
but they are singing it in the émigrés' cafés:
how good we are to cut the bourgeoisie's necks!
They are changing this words, of course.

2

At first, didn't you know,
during this revolution
they have some private enterprise
so a woman is selling bublyechki.
For this
Bublyechki
Give me roublyechki!

Bublyechki are like doughnuts
but more dense.

3

Why do you look like this for?
You think it is banal
for your European taste?
The picture, of course, is quite rubbish
but, I am afraid, for the tune
he took something from my soul.

A WEST COUNTRY TWIN TOWN

In the new year of our new life together
  When, dreamy, diffident
As stuttering English snow, we stole each other
  From history's Janus-glare,
And then, to cure our failure of intent,
  Glanced at a map, drove west

Towards the refuge of that kindest city—
  Fathered by Rome, but a true Hellenist,
Whose naiad waters, glorying in their own
  Warm, emerald climate, try to wash the frown
From marble rectitude: in that new year

A birch tree sidled up to welcome us
  Plaintively, a skinny city peasant
  Sighing the forest wasn't what it was,
And we, lounging in bed at noon, could count
  Through snow-dim glass a row
Of colonnades or pan-pipes, not convinced,
But happily suspecting that the pleasant
  Angel of English fantasy had swished
  Her wing across our view:
So we were held until the room went dark,
And vision sank to a shady glow of flesh . . .
  But midnight, scathing as a Bolshevik
Of love's imperial privacies, burst in
  And flung us out to public life again.

By one o'clock the city was a mess,
  Silent and slumped after the ritual shrieks
To *auld lang syne*, and dangerously chilled:
Even her dreams were limestone, moist and cold.

In that new year that wasn't a new start,
   Simply its shadow which, when lost,
Might still seem solider than all the rest,
   We watched grey water shrug itself along
In ruffled furs, and the mosquito snow
   Hugged by a ring of lamplight as it danced.
So deeply cold the sleeping city grew
   Each night that I believed her comatose,
Deaf to her naiads, fatally entranced.
   Even the Renault seemed about to die;
Curled like a mercury-ball, a frozen mouse,
It could not raise a spark, but coughed
   With wincing shoulders, frail, tubercular,
While, from your rag-bound thumb, a hot, red tear
   Was futile, like all human sacrifice.

I was prepared never to get away:
   Now that you'd told me where we might have been,
I'd come to think that it was where we were,
   And every street could float off into sea.

Your 'most-premeditated' city, scarved
   In tremulous rivers, numberless bloodstreams,
   And yet unable to escape its dreams,
Had locked us into one stern homesickness,
   So even when we freed ourselves, our roads
   Would always take us north, and Bath appear
In memory's closing window like the ghost
   Of Petersburg at the start of each new year.

THE FLOOD OF SILENCE

What killed Pushkin was not D'Anthes' bullet;
what killed him was lack of air.
BLOK

What a Devil's trick that I should be born
with a soul and talent in Russia.
PUSHKIN

On London nights, Decemberish, icy,
When streets and sky and Thames are all
One shimmering bale, gold-sequinned, pricey;
When the wind hardens to a wall
On corners where theatres glitter,
And words are tossed away like litter
While golden eggs lay pizza-chains
And burger-bars and video-games,
I think of you in Tsarskoye Selo
Writing your Ode to Liberty;
Bliss was it in that dawn to be
A dreamy, radical young fellow
Saved from Yakutsk, if not from court
By exile of a milder sort.

I think how silence spreads its rivers
Over unstable, swampy banks;
Even the bronze-wrapped horseman shivers
As bridges float away in planks.
A wave shins up a lamp-post's rigging;
First doors, then balconies are swigging
The muddy water, then the chimes
Of plump St Isaac's; on it climbs . . .
Miraculously, we can hear you
Still, as if you were a bird—

Art with an olive-sprig—absurd
Image that surely fails to cheer you
As you gaze out of Leningrad,
Your mausoleum, huge and sad.

You built your ark, although the rising
Flood was almost at your throat—
A speedy, shapely, un-capsizing
Twentieth-century language boat;
But still the future's uncreated
And writers with an elevated
Sense of buoyancy tend to drown

In deaths as airless as your own.
Brave actor, forced to play the gallant
When, in that proud, possessive place,
Adultery giggled in your face,
You died, having bemoaned your talent,
In shallow rivers of your blood—
Though you survive the greater flood.

CONVERSATION PIECE

(loosely based on a sketch from
Fragments of My Diary by Maxim Gorki)

Petrograd, 1918.
They stroll in the Summer Garden
Discussing whether the masses
Deserve an education—

One believer, one doubter
From the poles of the social classes,
Bound by the fond condescension
That writer reserves for writer.

They sit down under a tree;
The masses are swarming about—
Soldiers and shop-girls and sailors
Where the Romanovs walked on glass.

Only the gardener's unchanged,
Impassively slaying the grass
In the haemophiliac rosebeds
While the little Tsarevich stares,

Turning paler, paler, paler.
Gorki gets out his pipe.
Blok crushes a lozenge of sunlight
With an apocalyptic boot

And denounces, as is his habit,
The Intelligentsia's rôle.
Gorki the guttersnipe
Instantly loses his cool:

'The Intelligentsia drives
The engine of Progress. Your
Aristocratic contempt
Deserves a sock in the jaw!'

His cheeks shine tubercular red.
Blok looks at him strangely. The leaves
Of the ash tree scrape in his head
With a sound of puppet-strings, knives.

The smile of a passing laundress
Somehow changes the mood.
'Do you think there's a hope, old chap,
Of eternal life?' Blok mutters.

Cries Gorki: 'Of course it's eternal.
It's bloody miraculous
But everything's being recycled
Including the human race!'

'Listen. One late summer evening
Ten million evenings from this,
A shabby old pair of hacks,
Who should have something better to do,

Will be puffing out smoke and hot air
And explaining the Universe
As they sit on a bench and gaze
At a washer-girl's twinkling hips.'

Blok wrinkles his nose. 'You mean us?'
'Who else?' chortles Maxim, 'Who?'
Blok turns pale, be jumps up
In a fury of terror. 'You

Westernised heathen!' he shrieks.
'Thinking's the curse of the Slavs
And so I curse you and your granny!'
(Blok never does things by halves.)

Gorki sits calmly on,
Feeling sad for his fellow writer.
The young moon rises and glows
White as a peeled onion

And the stars shine brighter and brighter.
'Revolution! Eternity!
Mankind!' whispers Gorki. The gardener
Goes home for a glass of tea.

DEATH OF AN ELDER BROTHER

Stern-eyed Sasha, midnight reader,
Student of the worm,
Connoisseur of annelida,
How could he do harm?

Sasha spared his soily wrigglers,
Shunned the hook and knife.
But, said Sasha, Tsars are different
Lower forms of life.

There's a cause I'd gladly die for
Yes, and kill for too.
It's not natural, it's not moral
But what else to do?

Stern-eyed Sasha walks in leg-irons,
Clanking down the bight.
Ladoga laps, a workman taps
Out in the yard all night.

Sasha, Sasha, best Ulyanov,
Sobbed his brother, why
If you tried to save the people
Did you have to die?

In the young May dawn a broken
Life droops from a beam;
But the hempen rope binds stoutly
Dream to brother's dream.

Stern-eyed Sasha, midnight reader,
Student of the worm,
Connoisseur of annelida—
How could he do harm?

A MOSCOW WIFE, WAITING

Husbands wait sometimes, too:
But when I think of waiting,
I think only of you,

As if you were the true
Symbol of all waiting
And all who wait are you,

Larissa. And I see
The blackish lumps of snow
Surging to your dark porchway,

The flats in rows, the stairs
In hundreds, and I climb
Praying you'll be there,

Praying you won't be there.
I hear the clattered chains—
It's like a prison door.

You peep an inch. I'm scared
I've scared you—and just scared.
But then—I've stepped inside.

You sit and listen, pale
Distracted. You look ill.
The message falters. No,

It isn't much. I can't
Say much. And there's a word
Which you repeat and which

Baffles me. That it means
The most important thing
For you is all I know.

I'm sorry.' I bring out
My pocket dictionary.
The word is *amnesty*.

You said, 'I think there's hope.'
You didn't smile. I said
'I'm glad.' The words seemed small.

I took your hand, I went
Into the sleety cold.
And now I learn that hope

Was simply one more way
Of torturing you: they've sent
Your husband back to camp.

And yes, he's waiting, too;
But when I think of waiting
Somehow I think of you

As if you were the true
Symbol of all waiting,
And all who wait are you.

LENINGRAD ROMANCE

1. *A Window Cut by Jealousy*

Not far from the estuary's grey window
They lit cigarettes and talked. Water kept meeting stone,
Lips kept sticking to paper, time kept burning.
The lilacs were burning down to the colour of stone.
She said, I was born here, I've lived here always.
Stone kept moving in water, time kept burning,
Smoke became palaces, palaces faded and faded.
My home's in Moscow, he said, my wife and children . . .
Perhaps they are just the white ash-fall of night,
Perhaps they are stone. Stone kept looking at shadows,
Shadows died in the white ash-fall of night.
Water kept playing with windows, time kept burning,
Fingers played with the burning dust of the lilacs,
The palaces faded and faded. I've lived here always,
She said, I've friends in Moscow. Thoughts became palaces,
Time went out, hands became estuaries,
The estuary was the colour of dying lilac.
They talked and lit cigarettes. Shadows flowed over the table.
They fingered them, but they didn't notice mine,
Not far from the estuary's grey window.

2. *Safe Period*

He will unlock the four-hooked gate of her bra,
Not noticing a kremlin of patched cotton,
With darkening scorch-marks where her arms press kisses.
She will pull back her arms, disturbing drifts
Of shallow, babyish hair, and let him drink,

Breathless, the heavy spirit smell, retreating
At length with a shy glance to grasp the chairback,
And, slightly stooped, tug out the darker bandage.
Her cupped palm will glow as she carries it
Quickly to the sink, like something burning.
He sees the bright beard on each inner thigh,
Carnations curling, ribboning in the bowl.
Her hands make soapy love. The laundered rag
Weeps swift pink tears from the washing string.
He's stiffened with a shocked assent. She breathes
Against him, damp as a glass. A glass of red vodka.

A BLOCKADE MEMORIAL

There were platoons of tents, not one was closed.
Inside, in each wound's dark, we knew there'd be
Pale puzzles like ourselves: a flawed yorick

At last conversant with his mess of props.
But when we dared to peep, the ossuary
Held simply straw, the light dormition of roses

*

Since graves were everywhere, we couldn't see them.
The walkways bore them off to a last farewell—
A frayed red hand waving up from the ground.

We trod on oak-leaves, stars—the splashed confetti
Of giant brides. The verb 'to die' is vast—
A city. But 'to die for the motherland'

Has no visible end, works in all tenses,
State-like, and makes them present: there are always
Live feet going over and over the dead.

*

An east wind, solid with processional ghosts
Carrying brands that first lit glowingly,
Then blanched, the faces of the crowd, swept through us

And drove us to the gates, the sheltering temples.
They frowned in pity, gathering the shades
Into their smaller, denser, human forms.

*

Here stood a country looking for itself.
First it would find a baby's fist of bread—
The daily ration for 900 days—

And then, a diary. If the power lines ceased
Their faintest song, and tyre tracks, slithering,
Curved, for whatever reason, into silence,

If dry tongues ached against walls and shoe leather –
How could a diary speak?
Somewhere there are girls who still know how.

*

She was called Tanya. Round her once had lived
Her family. True to girlhood, courtesy,
She dipped her pen, listlessly, carefully;

As each one died, redeemed their gravelessness,
Making a loss-shape from the name and date
Until she had exhausted all her time

And reached her final name,
A child brought up to wait politely, take
The last turn in the complex grown-up game:

Everyone's died. Only Tanya's left.

*

Past the necropolis the earth lay snow-stilled
And empty, free to grieve in her own way –
Northerly, reticent. A concealed flood.

In moments were were tearless and absurd.
High-kicking, floundering through the half-whisked whites,
To storm the silver woods, our boot-tops foaming.

*

We found a pool. Dark water shivered thinly.
The adolescent birch trees seemed to step
Suddenly back, not liking to admit

How passionately they'd dwelt on their reflections.
Such slippages and slynesses and rumours!
We heard them, then: the ice-locks liquidly.

Yielding, the wind more westerly
With each gust. But the lost weight of the starving
Still drifted from the camps: who'd cup its grains?

Distant, triumphal chords kept touching us
Like old soldiers vaguely fingering
Their medals, asking why there's so much dust

On swept and watered stones. And spring, too young
To hear them, stoops to the tents with a light breath:
She wakes the roses, snips the bandages.

GREEN WINDOWS

Antarctica. Great plasterwork of gales.
The beach tumbled and whorled dull shades of white.
The surf a distant, quartzy heap of shale.

One step would crush the illusion. Underfoot
The relieved snow sank and fainted gushily.
More windows, glassy green, were breaking out

Each moment to the right and left of me—
For this was marsh, or would be, soon, a rippling
Of languid mosses mirroring the sea.

I became strangely homesick for the coupling.
I longed to breathe its salts across the warm
Midsummer midnight's pale, circadian riddle.

Instead, I would be guided dully home
By the same trail that brought me here, and plod
My own deep, swampy prints – the paradigm

Of the tourist trapped in ever-widening odds
Against a revelation. In that slow
Defeat, I paused and stared. A rain of buds

I'd missed before shone round me: pussy willow—
In any sky or language, Proserpina,
Eyes starred with sleep, and mellowing as a rainbow.

And now her promise soothed a hemisphere,
Carefree of borders, seeping, roaming, greening:
A wash of flowers left at an English door.

FINDING THE SUN

On Vasilievsky Island, brown and rumpled
With tramlines, stone in all its dreamed canals,
And plots still whispering through its plywood walls
I thought of the sun which Mandelstam had buried
In Petersburg, in the *velvet Soviet night*
And knew it lived, under the people's feet.

Wherever they trod, damp walkway planks or cobbles,
The crowds in their furry earflaps were trampling a thaw.
Rocks of soiled water loosened themselves
From the lips of drainpipes; soon, they'd dash for the river.
Spring's muddy pools would flower and the people know
That the time was ripe for exposing fragile earlobes.

In the meantime they went about hugged to themselves.
I thought of boats, their iron skirts swarming down
To the harbour-bed, lodging an iceberg's depth
Against a rusting anchor's mud-sunk sickle.
Dogged, they dreamed in queues, or butted the wind
Over bridges and through the arcades of Gostiny Dvor.

Darkness softly wrapped the great, flowing rush-hour
And still they were dawning and homing, those platoons,
Surging on their inscrutable manoeuvres.
They poured up from the burial pit of the metro
Like pyramid-builders, yoked by necessity.
Yet I saw how some had a secret happiness:

The militiaman in his heavy, mossy coat
Held a box of Napoleon pastry by its string
Daintily as a child's hand; a grey-faced woman
Lulled with her breath an armful of red carnations.
And in all the palaces rackety lifts crept up
Into night and the gleam of doors, bright-medalled with locks.

I sniffed a dialect, then, of *savoury pies,*
Pancakes, the evening samovar, soft sighs
And warm shawls and a hot stove to sleep on:
And the speeches lengthened, irremediable
In the lonely, jarring light of television –
But everyone wedged a chair in at the table.

Measured vistas, the seamless welding of Rome
And Byzantium in gold as thin as skimmed milk,
Cannot contain the skyline of their hope.
It sinks and flickers, looking for depth, for stone,
And this is the point it rests at. Vasilievsky—
Where the poets will meet again and find the sun.

THE ADMIRALTY

In the Northern capital, dusty *populus*,
Sighing, mantles the time's transparency,
And, through green dark, a frigate or an acropolis,
Brother to water and sky, glows distantly.

A boat of air, its mast like a touch-me-not—
To Peter's progeny, this rule declares
Beauty was never the whim of a demigod,
But a simple carpenter's calculating stares.

Four good elements rule us, but mankind
Is free; we've raised a fifth to pride of place:
Doesn't an ark so faultlessly designed
Repudiate the sovereign claims of space?

Cranky medusas consolidate a position,
Anchors' abandoned ploughs are adrift in rust,
But look, the three dimensions burst from their prison
And all the world's seas are open to us at last.

RUSSIAN LUCK

from the Russian by Yuri Drobyshev

I'm lucky. Russian-born, I think in Russian.
I eat my soup with bread instead of meat—
The Russian way. I dream and drink in Russian,
I even know the 'mother' oaths by heart,

Although I can't recall my actual mother.
I'm lucky. I've no friends. I feel no sadness
For anything on earth. I'm no one's lover.
I never fret about my circumstances.

If life is just, why should I start complaining?
What should I plead for if our needs are met?
Why should I sit behind the window, pining?
My day will come, the last and brightest yet.

Yes, it will come, that final, shining day
But, in the meantime, knuckle down, square up
And do the job. I'm lucky, certainly.
I wish my enemies this kind of luck.

PERSEPHONE IN ARMENIA

The snow was a blue lake in Pushkin Square,
A twist of streams down Tsar Alexander Boulevard.
Buds split against the greenish
Luminous sky, rare as Cuban dates.
It was warm, it was burning, it was spring!
The girl moved swiftly with her blood-fall.
She tore off her coat,
Laced on her chilly sandals.
We didn't have time to stop her.
She was racing up the hill
Where snowstorms were massing again,
Her bare legs white with winter,
Plaits sparkling like iced wheat.
And watched the afternoon
Turn pale with marriage.

We ride into our sunset,
Anonymous as exhaust,
Or a chainstore nightie,
Its wishful furbelows
Crushed, forgotten
Under the feather pillow
That won't be mine again.
But the postcards fly
In hot pursuit of us—
The borscht, so red
It ought not to be eaten;
A waiter who speaks Russian
Macedonian-style;
His following eyes,
Jealous as mine will be

When, drunk, you call him
Your brother Slav;
The flatly urban
Subjects you photograph
For sending home:
A used-car sale,
A hedge of scaffolding,
An entrance to the U-Bahn.
So what was there to see
At the border zone?
The defeated foliage?
The unimpressive watch-tower
Anyone could climb?
I lean from the platform
Trying to discover
From a gutted tenement
How you used to live
While you read a guidebook
In one of the mobile toilets
And occasionally groan.

Here I should modulate
To a distant key,
Surprise the hidden, grey
Sweetness of *Unter den Linden*
Satirise the two
Basilisks that stamp
Around the Gate.
There is a tour, of course,
But no earthly train
Driving into the iron
Teeth of that river
With the practised whoop
Of a border cavalier,

Could tear from it a promise
To give you back,
And I'm afraid
Some treacherous loneliness
Would wake in each of us
Were I to claim my privilege
And leave without you.

I take your hand instead
And in the spoiling air
Of mythic decay
Still breathed as liberty,
Still bought with blood,
We enter ritual
Like honeymooners
Swaying east
To watch the dawn break
Over Torremolinos.

It might indeed have been
Simply a wall—
Some usual, useless,
Surly, inner-city
Lump of municipal shit
The young had tried to claim.
I studied the slogans,
The painted names.
Now all I remember
Is 'We have smoked here'
The crimson Cyrillic
Rising clear out of all
That artful, artless writing
On our side of it.

from **Icons, Waves** (1986)

ICONS, WAVES

The scalding gulp that almost clears the glass,
love rushes to the human eye, and lends it
illusions of a focus so exact,
a driver might lurch out, steer straight to death.
But we, late diners who've got tired of dining
and turned to iconography, believe
inaccuracy is also revelation.
Under the broad lamp with its singing bulb,
we stare into each other's brightest stares,
unselfed with curiosity, archaic,
and paint each other in a universe
where nothing's lost by lying in perspective:
I have the details—red formica table,
rinsed baked bean tin with its clutch of spoons,
your flatmate's skinny plant, the sallow glitter
of our once quickly filled and emptied glasses.

•

It was a dangerous ship we put to sea in;
over-freighted, dressed in Baltic ice,
crewed by the breath-clouds that had been your story.
Burning hope like kerosene, it suffered
the magnets of exile, every wave.
And though we raised our glasses, splashed our beer
with the sly diminutive brewed for thirty degrees
of ideology and new-year frost,
our toast was the old harbour of Atlantis.
I'd come aboard for word trade, narrative,

warm money in my hand. You silenced me,
and it was then I felt the monster turn
his armoured intricacies under the waves,
and follow us like whispers, like ice.

•

So we'll be ageless, therefore timeless; so
we'll leave our heavy, fascinating shadows
on the doorstep; so, I said, we'll simply trace
in unobtrusive strokes what we are now.
You cracked the mystery fish, peeled the caul
from the red crayon of roe—which you gave me.
What part of taste, what part of time is this?
The bathrobe keeps slipping from my shoulders,
but we've been married silver years and gold—
a bare breast would neither shock nor rouse you.
Tell me their names—this fish, this salty planet,
so like and unlike earth, its bright omphalos
a kitchen table. Minutes ago we were strangers,
hours before that, lovers. It's two o'clock
I said in the new language; that's nothing, you said,
your mouth full of scales, that's children's time.

•

We slip into the darkest colour—stillness.
A half-sleep floats like tempera across
our pillows and our limbs, sunk on each other,
and in the dream that blooms from our alignment,
we wake into the rosy corner where
an icon flickers, wake into the icon.
On crimson cloth, the twenty chosen fingers
enact their imperfective verbs of touch.

The child's left hand clasps the maphorion
as it would a twist of hair; his mother's cheek
touches his, and one hand curves a cradle
for the small, uncertain spine; the other, raised,
hushes the infant universe. Dissolving
into one drowse of gold, these chosen heads,
these twenty fingers, can never say enough,
though laden with the silences of art.

•

The sun was like a diamond. Sleepily
while you worked nearby I tried to hold it
between my eyelids. All the birds were singing
to the sky's cold lavender. I slept again
letting you float—I trusted you to float
not far away. Such brightness trellised us
as if the iconographer had worked
in silver foil and gold, in pearl and turquoise.
The Virgin of the Don, like a czarina
in tear-drop gems and furry velvels, parted
the sky to smile. This was the world of money,
of purchasable grace. I woke and saw
your turned back, the diagrams spread out,
the lamp dipped as an aid to concentration
on slightly displaced, slightly obsolete fact.
Your small hand fetched the ruler in its mouth,
precise and happy as a little dog.
You squinted down and drew a swift straight line.

•

But space is curved, and all who sail in her—
plasmid, bacterium, foetus, curly brain,
the sea. Deep in each other's laps we slept,
well-matched for cradling. One shall never move
without the other, that's the law of nights.
The law of days is—one shall always move
while the other grasps, writhes up, sinks back,
sick as a sturgeon ripped from its spawing-ground
and flung in pouring silver on the heaped
and blushing deck. Only the sturgeon is luckier . . . —
it makes a single mistake.
We live to lift the glass again, to chase
the flying stillnesses, the mortal icons.

•

In the window lay blue light and other windows;
then there was only the print of this room
on glossy black, with a bare, sickle moon
that seemed to pierce me; now beyond the faint
kitchen glints as far as I can see
there is only black. I could be persuaded
that no moon exists, no trees, no windows
rooted in the round earth, no hope of daylight.
Patience, patience, say the little hearth-gods
smug on your hooks and shelves, unafraid of fire
or servitude—despair is simply one
point of view. And so I try again.
I imagine you travelling beneath the moon
I cannot see, I imagine you moving slowly
into this narrow frame. A greenish dawn
follows you, then the trees, the houses, daylight.

I imagine hope, and hope's redundancy,
our dark silhouette of reunion
an endless still that vanishes behind
the kissing curtains and the piecemeal snowfall—
after which there is nothing ever after.

•

She waited too; dawn did not bring you home.
Letters were sealed in tears, and crossed. One pleaded.
the other said – impossible. She froze . . .
The iron echo rings – impossible.
Something she'd read was happening to her:
a train pounding over the wooden bridge
over the frozen lake, and then its windows
slithering like a deck of yellowed cards
down through crashing struts, flames, slopes of ice.
The doors of the water closed. Your letters crossed,
sealed in freezing tears. Everything froze.
She stares up from the bottom of the lake.
The ice has healed smooth as lies, white-faced
as history. Impossible . . . yet you,
when I look down again, are lying there too.

•

This was my dream. You stood in the doorway
turning the dimmer-switch to a dark glow.
I saw the smiling boy, his butterfly-pause
in the shiny perspex trap, the matted gold
curtain-weave, the junk-shop paperbacks;
then, by the bed, your blue-bound Russian-English
slovar—a daring marriage
of words solemnly trying to mean each other,

telling their secrets in each other's arms.
I woke to the old standing-pool of dawn,
seeing only myself. The light changed,
shook with a breaking tremor . . .
You were beside me. So it's possible
to be happy, I said, and, in my dream,
I took your warm, lost body to my heart
and nursed my happiness to sleep again.

•

Minutes ago we were strangers . . . Now,
expecting my surprise, you fetch the *vobla*.
Have you forgotten the first taste you fed me?
Our tongues were stiffer, salt was sweeter, then.
You gesture doubtfully, intent on stripping
the fish to a few details of its life:
the papery, jointed pod of the swim-bladder
still tenderly inflated, twisting free,
and now the roe, delicately male
and seaweed-brown, not red as I'd imagined.
What part of light, what part of time is this?
Age, weariness, iconoclasm
watch us for our living salts, our rich
human skins . . .we swallow the drouth
till nothing's left beyond our lips but scales.
You wouldn't eat them, though I said so once,
wanting the pun, and your dear, careful mouth.

•

The boy, so harshly combed and tightly buttoned
into his miniature pin-stripes, looks up
with sparkling gaze and vague, milk-tooth smile,

all-trusting, though a tiny flinch betrays
his sudden, bright, important loneliness.
Somewhere off-camera you are watching him,
moving farther away but watching, watching,
till your eyes bleed with their attempt at filming.
Twenty years later, and you telephone
a birthday greeting, straining to receive
across a shower of crackling stars his tall
uncertain image, and to hear him smile.

•

There was another child, a child of wishes.
Long shadows had fallen, it was late,
but I saw him playing down by shallow water,
his language yours, diminutive, rinsed new.
For a moment, I thought you watched him too,
and the brightness in our eyes was double bright.

•

I am not the one.
Your fingertips understand it when they blindly
trace my short hair to a little below
the nape of my neck, no further.
I am not the one.
Still they trail onwards, smudging adored soft ghosts.
Dark were they, or light, or in-between?
Ringlets, or straight strands?
Your finger-tips could say, but so much knowledge
cannot translate to our shadow-language, thin
as the paper I write on. Without a past

we'll die to each other, ghost to ghost . . .
Your fingers mark the stony place.
They are human enough, they search for comfort,
but go on whispering: this is not the one.

•

Into the snowy east of consciousness
your dreams pull sledges, and your eyes are sealed
to keep the future from your wintering heart.
What's sourer than the after-taste of hope,
the nightly vodka at the wrong table,
the wrong attentive gaze? I think of those
who paid their one-way fare in useful lies,
the state turning a crass, wolfish cheek
on which a frail tear announced motherhood.
Is it freedom to forget the life you had,
or to carry it with you like necessity?
The west too is full of snow and whispers,
and if it were a woman it would say:
I had no choice but to disappoint you,
to become the cancelled myth, the ashamed silence,
a word that simply isn't in your language,
a foreign country, even to myself.

•

It was forbidden to destroy an icon.
Although, in time, the jewelled saints fell homesick
and dwindled smokily in mass ascensions,
their charisma remained, and only God,
sighing his aimlessness in moving water,
might wash and wash the remnant to pure nothing.

•

We too have left the life we dared not lose
on the vague strand where history runs in,
cold, innocent, light-fingered. *Goodbye*
until the next world, Zhivago sighed
heroically to his mistress, but we lack
such cheerful metaphysics. Time is all
we ever had: you scarcely treasure it,
and I can only lock it like the ghost
of the present-tense, into these antique rooms.
Better not to have tried to love at all,
perhaps, if this is the only world to love in,
and kinder never to have roused the child
we settled all those years ago to sleep,
if we did so merely to abandon it.
The names on streets, the names on playbills shone.
My bare arms earthed the sun. All that could burn
was you, in dreams more live than anything –
    my child, my ring.

from

From Berlin to Heaven (1989)

FROM BERLIN TO HEAVEN

2 *Munich*

Utopia—nowhere
I ever knew
Until that morning.
We had left the sleeper
Blackly streaming
South like an *anschluss*,
A riderless nightmare.
I was still wishing
Vienna, Vienna,
As her breath touched me.
She was pure city
And her brightening forth
In the moment between
Waking and blinking
The heavy gold-dust
Out of my surmise
Was familiar as only
A constant hope is.
We called her 'München',
Tender with surprise.

A sixties child
In a fire-touched brocade,
She curtseyed across
The Marian sky.
If she had willed
Her forgetfulness,
We couldn't blame her.

We too were wide-eyed,
We too, faintly poisoned.
As the day withdrew,
She possessed us differently.
Her shadow found you
And the catch in her voice
Was the buried grace-note
Of the Slav.

She turned and turned
Her Russian face
And I heard her whisper—
Extinguishing, enchanting—
Of divorce and marriage
It is divorce
Cuts the deeper heartline:
There can be no future
That is not his past.

Bound to this course,
One night we sat
In futurist Odeonplatz.
Islanded, water-dazzled
Lorelei,
We softly murdered
A song of the people.
Our thin strophes
Were the circles where
A mail-coach butterflied
With its snow-faced driver.
As the storm encrystalled
His upturned room

And kneeling horses
To the arched, brilliant silence
Of a polar tomb,
He dreamed a letter home
And his blood-sugar, sinking
Slowly to zero,
Saw him through
To the death-drowsy, solemn,
Last 'I kiss you'.

Perhaps the blur, stinging
Our eyes, was him.
Beyond us, too,
Lay distances,
Blanked by longing,
And, beyond these,
Expectantly
Fading towards us,
The radiance of footprints
We had each called 'family',
And betrayed.
And then I thought
Of a place too small
Even to spell,
A broken star
Where the map creased.
It blazed in the glare
Of an island's crime
Against her continent.
But we went on singing
Until history fell
In easy shadows

At the city's feet
And *peace in our time*,
Our breath said, peace
In our time.

3 *Democracy at the Burgerbraukeller, 1926, 1984*

We just walked in
And found the moment where
Enormous amber waves
Run beautifully over
The map of soiled empties
And history's remade.
Apprentice Hitler
Jumps on a table,
Trenchcoat-belt frisking
Like a clawed, clumsy tail.
He shoots the ceiling—
A Michelangelo
From the heavy suburbs
Where art is caricature.
Stage dandruff sifts
Onto uniforms, suits.
The patrons still don't know
Whether salvation dances
In such smeared boots.
They study surfaces
Especially those that wink
And brim their glasses—
Worth ninety Marks a sip.
When the order comes
To carry on drinking,

Up go a thousand suns.
The chairs scratch and clap
The floorboards' backs,
And full throats roar
How they will always be
For hops and barley
Whoever's yelling 'Time'
At the pantheon
From below an aproned lip.
He shrinks a little now.
He's almost Chaplinesque
But not incredible
(And not quite charmless)—
His glance could quickly pierce
Us where we sit.

5 *David*

His home was in Tel Aviv
but he didn't mind West Berlin
where he'd lately been appointed,
'in the spirit of atonement,'
Writer in Residence.
He wasn't writing.
He showed us, instead,
The new watercolours,
Rainy, soft, Northern.
His poems had translated
To something brighter-lit.

Though we never quite said
The words he wished to hear
He treated us for dinner
At the *Grosse Mauer*.
Service was ponderous
As a Brahms adagio
Carved with a chopstick
In Chinese granite.
We sat like our starched napkins—
You, depressed and shy
Because you thought us closer
Than was the case—
We, platitudinous
In the scoured EFL
We felt we had to use,
Both far too courteous
To meet. To live.
He wrote in Hebrew, dreamed
(He said) in Yiddish,
Got by in German,
Remembered Polish,
But now he was worn out
And best at silence.
He feared the path of words
In any forest.
Too many branches threw
Deranging darkness there.

The other day I found
An early book of his,
Opened it at this:
When they call my name

With a Slav accent
It's as if my mother were calling me
To the Sabbath meal.
And I stood still,
Dismayed that we had missed
Something so simple,
Needing only your voice
At its most artless
To tender and release
The familiar shadow,
Spread it at his feet,
Pale with the bloom of snow.
First he would pause and then
See the window change,
The moving, dark mass,
Sheened by candle-light,
Turning into a face—
Young, unmarked, long-dead
That laughed, that let him in.

7 *Masada*

There was one god
Too huge to bury.
We crawl in his frown.
Its lumps and pleats
Ache against
A small, cruel sun.
If sacrifice
Is necessity
And we honour those
Whose blood was teased out

Like a tress of crimson
River from rock,
Should we admire
A truck or plane
That assumes the form
Of a burning bush?

Our cable car
Shivers, sinks.
Better to say
We're in god's hands
Though his fingers are nothing
But wings and prayers.
We're looking down
On an aftermath:
The sleepy lips
Of the dunes parting
Over steel thumbs:
Transfiguration's
Eye-blink, then
An ash of visions
Where the sky touched Gehenna,
Where we were human
For the last time.

The earth is sweet
But a tar path
Sends us in scalded
Leaps to the sea
And that grainy chair
Is comfortless
As Jordan's arm
Round Israel's shoulder.

Seraphim walk,
Piercing, careless,
All over us.
We hang and hear
The tablets gasp
As a flung bottle
Bursts with commandments:
To be soul
To be salt
To be sky
To be skin—
To be stripped of it.

WEALTH

One Christmas we'd have said 'Rovaniemi'
And bounced in lightly on an Arctic tail-wind
To see the sleigh parked on the airport roof.

I would have steadied you on your first skis
Between the clotted fields, and sent you sailing,
Inarguable brightness overhead,
The clean, etched groove ice-hard in front of you.

RIDES

The enraged father,
His new romance on the skids,
Yells 'Get out of the car!'
The daughter stumbles out:

'I'm going, don't worry!'
But her fury dissolves quicker
Than his tail-lights can bleed
Away down the Mile End Road.

She's back to square zero.
She had her bag with her, packed.
She was happy. She was going home
And now she's not.

She sits against a door,
One elbow on the bag,
One tube of Tennent's in her hand.
She keeps telling herself to move on,

But only her mind moves . . .
Like this boy she vaguely knows,
Might pull in beside her.
'How you doing?' he says.

'Fancy a drive?'
They head for the motorway.
'I hate my dad,' she says.
'All I did was tell him

His girlfriend's mental.'
'North or West?' the boy asks.
'Alton Towers or Stonehenge?'
She chooses North. She sings

And now she's shrieking
Upside down and his arm's
Strong and the music's loud;
Even his armpit smells good.

This is all she needs to be happy . . .
But the Towers are closed, stupid
And they put a fence round the Stones
And stoned the hippies . . .

She wakes with the sharp dawn light
Trying to get through her eyelids,
Weaving jazzy black into red
Like something to cover a settee.

Trucks are lifting her hair
On their stream. Her body's pavement:
She's got to break each bit
To sit up, to find out

If she can walk. She feels robbed.
She could have been raped, so much
Is aching, so much is empty.
She's not got a dream left

About boys or cars or fun
Because all bloody England's wrapped up,
Fenced off, there's nowhere to go
And not be taken for a ride.

JARROW

Nothing is left to dig, little to make.
Night has engulfed both firelit hall and sparrow.
Wind and car-noise pour across the Slake.
Nothing is left to dig, little to make
A stream of rust where a great ship might grow.
And where a union-man was hung for show
Nothing is left to dig, little to make.
Night has engulfed both firelit hall and sparrow.

ABOVE CUCKMERE HAVEN

(for John Bunzingham)

This is a reachable coast:
The cliff, though it unscrolls
The modest curve of a buttress,
Is no young Atlas
And doesn't presume to try
Shouldering up the sky—

And the sky itself,
Translucent as a harebell,
Pales, but will not disclose
The point at which it wavers,
Becomes an immortelle
Of gases, stars.

The forsaken pillboxes
Doze in their rust,
No patriotic gull
Wooingly calls
The farm-boys to enlist;
Though the air seems prodigal

With ghostly fires again,
These are the grandchildren
Who never went to the Somme,
Dunkerque or Spain,
But packed the silos dumb
With missile-grain.

Visions, like meadow-blues,
Are dust in the hand,
Seed where the grass thins
To light, and where the cliff
Perishes, chalk and sand:
This is a coast of bones.

What remains is a view:
The cliff, upswept from the beach
And the drying threads of the mere,
Lifting whitely two
Crumbling wings, on which
Other wings briefly appear.

THE FIRST STROKES

Letter to a friend learning English

Before he died, my father drowned in silence.
I thought of him just now, writing to you
In my head about the sea – that medicinal light
I longed to rush to your city of rooms and deadlines,
Your lost July – since it was he who taught me
To swim. In any sea he was stylish, fluent.
He knew its idioms, loved its argument.
So, when my four-year-old, his adventuring grandchild,
Slipped her hold on a wet rock, dropped speechless
Into the swell, he plunged and rescued her.
She used to tell us how huge fish came leering,
Making eyes at her as she bubbled down;
Now what she likes to remember are the hands
That drove apart the soupy green, and calmly
Scattered her suitors, saved her for the sun.
It was soon after this I led him to the pool:
I made him teach me. And, in half an hour,
I had left his side, was lazily at home
In the deepest water, thinking I'd always known how.
It was as simple as doing what he told me—
An obedience I could never risk as a child.
By the time he lost language, I had almost learned
To talk to him. He studied dictionaries
At first with an embarrassed grin, then frowning,
And the deep words we could have plumbed together
Ran white. I thought of all this, writing a blue
Letter about the sea, wanting to coax you
Into the tongue you almost know, but fear,
Having come so late to its stories; wanting to say

That the strokes of an English sentence are easy, requiring
Only a little self-trust as you kick off
From the margin and glide towards me, sensing all round you
The solid, patient, unbreakable arm of the water.

THE MARCH OF THE LANCE-BOMBARDIER AND HIS CHILDREN

The road is stopped with corners; darkness moves
All round us like a forest of blue soldiers.
To walk much farther needs a sense of purpose
Beyond the iron love of feet for world.
There are no villages, not a single cottage.
No lights. Yet everybody takes this road.

The mountains have been blinded and let loose
To wander where they like among the planets.
The waterfalls are only storms of ashes,
The loch a vast slate from the tumbled sky.
No headlamps stare, no burning stubs of cat's-eyes—
And that's why every driver heads this way.

We turned back for the only certain shelter
(Or so we thought)—the one we'd started out from
In flares of sodium, gassy as champagne,
To plunge into the flute-pure black of pine trees,
Our torch blanching the rain: yes, we turned back,
While you, with ghostly footsteps—you kept walking.

Was it good, sometimes, to march in uniform
In clouds of human breath between the mountains?
Perhaps it almost felt like solitude
With Ursa Major's posed, angular brilliance
Above your head, more pin-up than Great Bear
And other ranks and stragglers, melting nowhere?

You passed us miles ago, we merely saw you
Vanish. Now you must have turned all comers,
Silenced all waterfalls, and reached at last
The garrison town, to wait for further orders.
Something will happen; something always happens.
You steel yourself for the pitching sea-road: France.

Or else you're only dreaming of it all.
Men can nod off, you said, while on the march.
Their eyes close while their feet, on auto-pilot,
Cleave to the old rhythm of the road.
I didn't ask you if they dreamed as well;
But now I'm sure dreams are inevitable.

You lay your kit out by the barracks window;
You brasso every button till it burns
And waters into stars and leafy sunlight.
You swim the green Ardennes; float back, still sleeping;
Begin to darn your heavy marching sock.
The needle stumbles brightly, pricks your finger.

Your eyes jump up, salute the road again.
All round you is black Scotland, men and pine trees
Marching as they breathe. Without agreement
Or argument, they haul the sullen load,
And each turned corner pays out a new length
Of dark. Yet everybody takes this road.

RECONSTRUCTION

The Dietrich Bonhoeffer Kirke
had no name to me then
in nineteen-fifty.
A tall meat-coloured ruin,
it was perpendicular
but dead-eyed, hemmorrhaging
bricks and secret rainbows
in the thickening leafage.
My father told me
it would stand like this forever
to teach the Germans.
As we climbed the wooden bridge
over the railway
I kept looking around
more and more dizzily,
garbling the fact
of cloud with retribution
till a whole fleet glowed there
like cherubim,
each pilot forced to gaze
down through the smoky nimbus
of his last mistake.
Was there truly a pact
between God and ourselves
to hold them eternally
in the sky above Dacres Road
even as they burned
ashen with their planes?
Modest in victory,
I felt their shame, and turned
instead to watch the trains.

PERESTROIKA

This is my sadness—
To have been the future
You thought you wanted.

This is your sadness—
That the most astonishing future
Began without you.

LATE TRAVELLERS

Your antiquarian friend
Shows you a perfect city
On its death-bed of water.

October smoke has stolen
Into the dying hair
Of my lover.

He never touches me now.
The curves of my body do not move him.
There is no language for this.

It weighs on me simply, like exhaustion.

BHEIR MÉ O

The night, that traditional
Short cut, where friendly
Differences meet,
Roving instinctively
In the foot-hallowed places,
The air familiar
And dense and fragrant
As they push it gently nearer
Each other's faces,
Is overgrown by sea
And strangeness now,

A permanent travelling tide
Of long black shadows,
Bright-edged and cold,
Where we, with cancelled senses,
Timidly wade,
Not knowing whose lamp, if any,
Stretches its fingers
In hope or in mimicry
Of hope, from the other side.

from **Thinking Of Skins**

(1993)

ST PETERSBURG, RECLAIMED BY MERCHANTS

The wind was terrorising the simple river,
Smacking the wobbly flesh about its waistband.
Pushkin, the tourists thought, looking tenderly down
At the curled green lip, the slurping meal.
The locals stared at a different kind of moral.
Flood was a long word in a poem they'd learned
At school. Now they were learning grown-up things:
How much to ask for a papier mâché icon
Stolen by someone's cousin, how not to be sold
Down the metaphorical river, and other secrets
Dark as the dark-eyed bride the matchmaker brings.

SEASCAPE AND SINGLE FIGURE

It isn't the seagulls, whitened
Lecterns of rock or wind,
Whose cries make the heart cry,
But those who scatter delinquent
Footprints, feathered with sand,
As the visible evidence that children fly.

My shadow, askance and pale,
Crosses the beach, with me:
We sit on the spread towel,
Folded together complicatedly
As a marriage or Swiss Army knife.
So the shadow is one with the life.

Nearby, a village is settled
With windbreaks, push-chairs.
Children gather and build.
The candid embodiment of
The most popular version of love,
They are the day's, its flush, its goldening, theirs.

And disinheritance
Is the sea, burnt almost to nothing,
A chemical, austere,
Standoffish radiance
Sending a few thin waves, slow-lathering,
Choked, to encrust the shore.

What does it matter if less
Than a dazzled moment ago
I swam with the warmer flow?
Those choices, that lack of choice,
That enviable sorrow,
Are not renewable.

Bright as crayoned sunshine, still
The coast-train winds among
The drifted crowds, pouring them out like grain
From a summer which, for so long
Disguised as a miracle,
Empties only to fill and brim again.

LAST OF THE LAYS

Part One

At Ivalo's tyre-crazed crossroads, snow was the sphinx
And *Murmansk* was what she murmured. One night you got restless.

(The nights were long, alas. We weren't new lovers.
'Follow me. I am your Fate' wouldn't wash any more.)

I heard your foot-swords slicing the forest-fleece
With finality. Then from your breast swooped a brilliant birdman.

Choice, choice, choice gasped the wind as you gashed it.
In front of you, ghostly as lilacs, stood your live lungs.

Part Two

In Persil-white Ivalo the enemy was drink.
I had nothing to come to but a Finnish Cosmo

And nothing to read but a radioactive omelette.
My cutlery stuttered, my skis would begin any minute,

So I tacked outside into a mean minus-thirty,
And wound up at the Word, that high-lettered horror.

I turned as it told me. I plummeted and plodged
And became wildlife and expected instant extinction.

I lit on the luminous secret of synchronised movement
Momentarily, but omitted to take it with me.

I slept on my skis, and revolutionary roughnecks
Lobbed snow lumps like one-off hand-jobs, and roamed the ice

Like spinning-tops wreathed in a frost of eye-water.

Part Three

Bang on the border, they'd opened a Super-Safeways,
Hit by recession, closed for the duration.

Some tanked-up gun-jabber jogged me: 'Nadezhda Krupskaya?'
'Crumbs!' I said. 'Wrong revolution. Julian Clary.'

Part Four

He didn't find that funny, which meant, as I'd feared,
History hadn't happened, it hadn't begun.

And though the ski-tracks still straggled under the *Push* sign
They were being disexisted at serious speed.

This was the hairiest I had ever imagined:
Me, on God's side, just about. You, back on the other:

The border, bristling. Remember those terrible games—
When the sound's switched off, there's got to be someone dancing,

And the grin's de rigueur, because English losers are laughers?
I hope, wherever you're harboured , you look like a natural—

Straight bck, heels tgthr, bm on chr –
I hope when it thaws and the home-thoughts unfreeze our faces,

Whoever I am I'll
                    author an honest tear.

ENGLAND TO HER MAKER

Hephaestus we tried to tell you
the signs were everywhere
you kept your head down

face to the glare
hammering bevelling punching
all that noise and smoke

no wonder you didn't hear
you were wreathed in the heat
and darkness of your craft

never stood upright
except to hammer our silences
with ringing cries of grievance

peculiar to your class
eyes clearer than yours Hephaestus
were noting the lack of new orders

we don't deny you had skills
you armed the fighting gods
invented such curiosities

as the self-propelling tripod
the fire-breathing bronze bull
magnificent yet not

exactly what life's about
any more we have microchips
we have genuine automation

quiet machines that can reason
unlike your rough irons
clanking brainlessly filthily

think of your lungs black
as the grass round here your legs
bowed under you like pliers

you could have a job sitting down
somewhere warm and well-lit
where there's music plants fountains

imagine yourself with white cuffs
tapping a keyboard smiling
taking credit-cards only smiling

it's the future you can't fight the future
you can't argue with progress
Hephaestus look at it this way

MIDNIGHT

(i.m. Jerry Orpwood, 1942-88)

The day was a difficult child.
Now it's fallen asleep,
You can hear yourself breathing
Evenly, without fear.

The emptied hour-glass shines,
Sealing the last room,
The last absence, like a mirror.

Why should you turn it over?
At this moment only
The silver pathway lies
Open at your feet.

It will mount the stairs with you
And unfurl into the stars,
Their distant dream-school.

Stretch your hand to the light-switch,
Press your face among feathers,
The soft pen-nibs scratching
A peaceful nonsense.

Think dizzily of the tilt
Of the world again, the weight:
How its dark sands are massing
To drop another day.

STEALING THE GENRE

It was the shortest night of the year. I'd been drinking
But I was quite lucid and calm. So, having seen her
The other side of the bar, shedding her light
On no one who specially deserved it, I got to my feet
And simply went over and asked her, in a low voice,
If she'd come to my bed. She raised her eyebrows strangely
But didn't say 'no'. I went out. I felt her follow.

My mind was a storm as we silently crossed the courtyard
In the moist white chill of the dawn. Dear God, I loved her.
I'd loved her in books, I'd adored her at the first sighting.
But no, I'm a woman, English, not young. How could I?
She'd vanished for years. And now she was walking beside me.
Oh what am I going to do, what are *we* going to do?
Perhaps she'll know. She's probably an old hand—
But this sudden thought was the most disturbing of all.

As soon as we reached my room, though, it was plain
She hadn't a clue. We stood like window-displays
In our dawn-damp suits with the short, straight, hip-hugging skirts
(Our styles are strangely alike, I suppose it's because
Even she has to fight her comer in a man's world)
And discussed the rain, which was coming down, and the view,
Which was nothing much, a fuchsia hedge and some trees,
And we watched each other, as women do watch each other,
And tried not to yawn. Why don't you lie down for a bit?
I whispered, inspired. She gratefully kicked off her shoes.

She was onto the bed in no time, and lay as if dumped
On the furthest edge, her face—dear God—to the wall.
I watched for a while, and, thinking she might be in tears,

Caressed the foam-padded viscose that passed for her shoulder,
And begged her not to feel guilty. Then I discovered
That all she was doing was breathing, dead to the world.

It wasn't an insult, exactly, but it was a let-down—
And yet I admired her. Sleep. If only I could.
I rested my hand at an uncontroversial location
South of her breasts, maybe North, I don't remember,
And ached with desire and regret and rationalisation.
I'd asked her to bed. And she'd come to bed. End of story.
Only it wasn't the story I'd wanted to tell.
Roll on, tomorrow, I urged, but tomorrow retorted:
I'm here already, and nothing ever gets better.

But then, unexpectedly, I began to feel pleased.
To think she was here, at my side, so condensed, so weighty!
In my humble position (a woman, English, not young,
Et cetera) what more could I ask of an Irish dawn
Than this vision, alive, though dead to the world, on my duvet?
What have I done to deserve her? Oh, never mind,
Don't think about words like 'deserve'. So we lay in grace.
The light. Her hair. My hand. Her breath. And the fuchsias.
I thought of the poem I'd write, and fell asleep, smiling.

I woke in a daze of sublime self-congratulation
And saw she was gone. My meadow, my cloud, my aisling!
I could hardly believe my own memory. I wanted to scream
All over the courtyard, come back, come to bed, but how could I?
She might be anywhere, people were thick in the day
Already, and things were normal. Why are things normal?

I keened her name to the walls, I swam bitterest rivers,
I buried my face in the cloth where her blushes had slipped
And left a miraculous print that would baffle the laundry:
Oh let me die now. And the dark was all flame as I drank
The heart-breaking odour of Muguets des Bois and red wine—
Hers, though I have to admit, it could have been mine.

COLD DAWNS

1 *Nightmare*

Busy as paddles in liquid, ratchets in clocks,
   An army is making new clouds above the Falls,
   And the rain-thin quilt we wear for rest unravels
And some are lulled, some trapped behind rattled locks,

And none can wake. Adrift in the bickering flow,
   That fills my kitchen with questions, still asleep,
   I pick up my kettle, tum, and almost leap
From the drawn blade flashed across the dawn-dark window.

2 *Maryville Avenue*

The frayed orange rug of a single lamp
Covers most of the street. Awake already,
The cement-works pants like a thirsty taxi.
The sky is one shade lighter than the tarmac,
But ghostly, still, in night-colour. Night-cold
Blooms in my doorway, solid with amazement.
The shiny, tidy dark of all I can see
Like the child's address—house-number to universe—
Or the confident water-rings of a thrown pebble,
Ends nowhere, has no end. How little the world is.
How it touches at every point, since your footsteps died across it.

SCHOOLGIRL'S STORY

The news stayed good until Monday morning
When a taxi-driver was shot in the South of the city,
And his un-named schoolgirl-passenger injured.
Outside the window, clouds made changeable bruises
And spillings. Bad weather, taxi weather.
I picked up my dish, poured everything down the sink,
unclogged it with bare fingers, ran for my coat,
Played back a dream of how it used to be,
Hearing about these things every day of the week
And not feeling cold and sick and hot: the beauty
    Of being nobody's lover.

I could hardly breathe as I reached the school railings.
The clouds turned heavy again, opened fire
On my face and eyes with stinging rice-grains of hail.
Bad weather, taxi weather. *If it's not there*
I'll run, and my screams run with me, from here to Balmoral.
But the bike was on its stand in the shed as usual.
The square-root of the frame, graceful, ice-blue,
Cut me the old two ways: her nearness, her distance.
The sky paled. I began to look for her
Without seeming to. I stopped feeling sick for her.
    Another sickness took over.

THE LISBURN ROAD LIST

(Variation on a Theme of Philip Larkin)

Glooms of old stone between shops,
And flat oases that blaze
All night, as ubiquitous
As copywriters' full-stops;
Churches and garages, both, in their different ways
Telling us this is a road going somewhere else:

And the buses to *Silverstream*
Via Shankhill, crowded as far
As the bone-hard, low-church seats
Punishing each rear,
And the dozens of other competitive notions of 'home',
And the eyes gazing carefully down on each 'somewhere else':

And the dusks, as mornful and slow
As the queue at the road-blocks,
A fire-engine screaming through,
Past the heavily-macintoshed barracks,
And the passers-by and the drivers thinking 'what's new?',
Thinking 'Jesus Christ, why don't I live somewhere else?'

And the gentler fantasies
For sale—a new colour-scheme,
Facials, cheap holidays,
And, if all else fails, an ice cream;
And the intricate, well-worked hills undeceived by the dream
That life could be utterly different, somewhere else.

And at last the ephemeral I,
Observant or bored, but never
Doubting that summer will soon
Arrive to unveil a vast sky
Of rooftops and trees and the hard bright light of that question:
Where is your love for the life you had somewhere else?

SNOWFIRE

The chimney stacks had been variously feathered
As the north wind pushed across Maryville Avenue,
Whitening a corner here, a full side there,
And sometimes leaving the odd stack disregarded.
The roofs were white, the clouds a little less so.
They moved on fast, as if from the scene of a crime
They'd merely witnessed, but would be accused of.
At first, I thought it was only chimney-smoke
From a late-night hearth, trying to join the cloud-rush.
Then came a flashing, lit from beyond the apex.
Something on fire? It was bright enough, but silent:
A fire can't work without muttering, carelessly
Giving itself away. And now the wind
Was gushing up and up, and the roofs were dissolving,
And all the street was fainting and dazzling itself
In the fumey blast. I watched till my face went under,
The fire wanted in, and I had to shut the door.

HEAD COLD

River-mouth world, is it really a surprise
That a new tenant has judged your sinuses
An ideal home? Your breath aches through his coal-smoke—
Smell of the ancient tenderness of cities—
His fumey speeds sicken you like catarrh.

So many clouds, heroes of stone and shell—
The loveliest headache, if you could bear to look;
Every street laid with a different carpet,
Each garden its own mist of imagined spring,
Though a gloved thumb could wipe out any petal.

Strange city, doped and bright in your frosty vest,
Keep to your bed today, and fall in love
Again and again with the childhood illnesses
When your hands, unusually clean, turned the pages
Of adventures you could not possibly have.

IN MEMORY OF A FRIENDSHIP

Winter has reached the Spanish Steps, advancing
On tides of dirty suds like the landlady
Who mopped her way past literature, enticing
Tubercle bacilli from every mouse-hole.
The red street-carpets, swaggering muddily
Persuade the tourists to the Latin Quarter.
Hawkers, pipers, backpackers, gypsies, thieves,
Unabashed by the civic or the tonal,
Go on arguing as they've always done.
If someone's down to his last adjective,
Why should they care, among all these words and rain?

Joseph takes the day off for gardening.
He'd mentioned violets, and his friend forgot
The taste of coughed-up rust, fed on their sweetness.
The gifts seem lame, now, curiously weightless,
Loveletters to a sickbed, crushed unopened.
His own hand clenches, but he crowds the plot.
The buds twist on their necks to look at him,
Measure his skewed perspective, his unquickened
Muse. These were his painting-days. The rest
Is a double-grave, much visited, but modest,
The young men in it sharing, like two students,
Who think they've all their fame ahead of them.

Now sunlight soothes the convalescent steps
Where the tourists never leave, but simply swap
Countries, friends and occasionally, their jeans.
Epiphany's over, and the filthy carpets
Rolled and trucked away to be drycleaned.

The landlady mops the hall again, re-lets
The rooms to the one tenant who'll never leave.
The rooms learn to be quiet. But youth can't learn.
It takes offence at barely lived-in bones,
Watches, distraught, its ownerless name become
Less than the rain, less than the grave that drowns
Each spring, in earth-rich violets, acts of love.

THE RELEASE

When the plane lifts for the last time in the damp, grey, tender air
Over the small fields neatly swirled with mowing-furrows,
The Friesian cattle jumbled like dominoes
By their rusty outhouse, I shall take one harsh breath
And fall instantly to dust, a thousand years old
Like the sybil freed from the curse that had kept her from dying.

from **Best China Sky** (1995)

DISTANCES

When she falls backwards and meets the fire and the rain,
Last of her generation in this absurdly continent family,
Who will remember her, make a note of her overwhelming virtues,
And colourful evasions: who will truthfully describe
The face that always remained a stubborn child's,
Outstaring us with hardiness, impudence, fear:
Who will follow that stare to the father:
Who will stand at the grave and tell him she was hurt:
Who will show the mother and sister what they stole:
Who will ask the young man, disappointed and disappointing,
For one of those Valentine poems she smiled at and soon mislaid
(The ever-blue handwriting knotted with shyest self-declaration):
Who'll untangle the whiteness and free all the numerous shapes of
    her lips?

They will say, those greatest of aunts, those most-removed cousins
Whose names she almost remembered, that it's not up to them
Since she leaves a child: this is the child's business.

Don't look at me. I'm innocent. I'm not the one
To speak of the dead. I can't even speak to the living.

FROM THE ANGLO-SAXON

Visit me again, one of these evenings.
Bring the gift of your small self, wisely hooded in wool,
The cold-blush winging your face, your eyes all flight.
Let my shadow befriend your slowly settling shyness.
Come without being called, without first calling.
I'll have the coal bright, the bottle cold, in no time.
Tap at my door, my window, I'll welcome you always—
I, who rise helplessly when the hollowest fingers
Flutter and flap at the letterbox-flap, let it go.

WAR AND SOUP

(i.m. Georgi Valentinovich Drobyshev, 1907-1995)

Rear Admiral (retired)
Of the Soviet Fleet,
Your father, wearing
His soiled cook's
Babushkin halad,
Manhandles down
From its several hooks,
The ticklish weight
Of the Samurai sword.
Losing no face
To the chopping board,
It flashes before you
What it did in the old days,
And still might do
If it weren't a ploughshare.

In a distant kitchen
Forty years later,
You recall the scare.
Sand-speckled mortars
Rear up for food
As we watch the slow fade
From suits to bellicose
Huddles of khaki.
There was a peace plan:
'Our hopes are high' . . .
Now I want to cry
Oh, let me see
That old sleight-of-hand—

Catastrophe twirled
To the windfall or wedding
Where good stories end!
But the telly glows
And roars. War wins.

The Samurai Chef
Keeps humming a tune
In your home-grown *skazka*.
He shifts a serene
And fabulous grip
As the sword makes deft
Green lacework of each
Noble napper.
Then he gathers the threads,
Lets them whirl and skip
In his own fairy tale.
When the rumour is rich
Enough, he'll announce
The feast, and share,
Golden, unbloodied,
His bequest of soup-moons.

Even now, our spoons
Could kiss the breathing bowl.

THE BORDER BUILDER

No sooner had one come down
   Than he began building again.
My bricks, O my genuine bricks
   Made of my genuine blood!
What would we be without borders?
   So which one are you? he said
And stuck out his hand to me.
   Birth certificate? Passport?
Which side are you on, which side?
   Merrily he unrolled
Starry dendrons of wire
   To give his wall ears and eyes.
Qualifications? he said.
   Residence permit? Tattoo?
Which colour are you, which colour?
   No colour, he said, no good.
He took my only passport,
   He slammed it down on the wire.
My hand, O my genuine hand!
   This is a border, he said.
A border likes blood. Which side's
   Your bloody hand on, which side?

BEST CHINA SKY

A primrose crane, a slope of ochre stacks,
Stencilled on tissue-thin
Blue, and, flung between
These worlds, a sword-flash rainbow,
The cloud it lies against,
Metallic as its topmost skin,
And, round the eyes of hills,
The tender bluish-green
That quickly yellows.

The prism comes and goes:
Wonderful stain, transparency of art!
A smoke-wraith sails right through it.
But now it strengthens, glows and braves its span,
You'd think it was the rim
Of some resplendent turquoise plate,
Offering hills and cranes and streets and us
Fancies designed to melt
As our fingers touched them.

PRAYER FOR BELFAST

Night, be starry-sensed for her,
Your bitter frost be fleece to her.
Comb the vale, slow mist, for her.
Lough, be a muscle, tensed for her.

And coals, the only fire in her,
And rain, the only news of her.
Small hills, keep sisters' eyes on her.
Be reticent, desire for her.

Go, stories, leave the breath in her,
The last word to be said by her,
And leave no heart for dead in her.
Steer this ship of dread from her.

No husband lift a hand to her,
No daughter shut the blind on her.
May sails be sewn, seeds grown, for her.
May every kiss be kind to her.

DEATH OF AN AFTERNOON WOMAN

Something is pushing them
To the sides of their own lives
PHILIP LARKIN, 'Afternoons'

A hand, was it? Or something heavier,
Swooping with the downswing,
Its shoes packed with meat
And little bones chipped from my own?
At first I didn't resist:
I'd be kicked anywhere,
Sit smiling on the farthest seat.
Was life mine to be lived?
Almost against my will,
As the chain-swings swooped, I heard
The seas divide.
I was walking a paper stillness,
A perfect centre parting
Through the roar of weather.
My life? Thanks. I'll rhyme it.
I'll keep it.
Keepers losers, they whispered
And I woke up.
If this is my house, it's mist,
If this is my land, water,
Constantly traversed
By miniature heels, child hands,
Wide open, chainless.
The force I feared is so small,
I could catch it in a caress
And run with it to wherever
It tells me our home is.

FROM A CONVERSATION DURING DIVORCE

It's cold, you say, the house.
Yes, of course I'll go back one day,
Visit, that is. But the house

Will be cold, just as you say.
Two people have left home,
One of them me, and one

Our youngest child. So of course
It's cold, just as you say,
And big, too, bigger at least

Than it was with everyone there.
Don't think I don't think about you
Being cold in a house that size,

A house that gets bigger, too,
And colder each time I dare
Think about you and the house.

It used to be warm in the days
Before I decided to go,
And it didn't seem big at all,

In fact, it was rather small,
Which is partly the reason I . . .
Don't keep on asking me why

And telling me how it is
In the house. I don’t want to know.
How can I go back, how can I

Even visit a house that size,
And getting bigger each minute
With all the cold rooms in it?

THE RESIGNATION

The mother we were free to hate is dead.
The last we saw of her, her face was breaking:
Only the palace of her hair still stood.
Her sons threw off their sullenness and cheered.
Her daughters, too, denied their hearts were aching.
We knew she'd leave us nothing. She loved men,
Next to herself, and we were none of hers.
Bur, yes, we thought her of some consequence—
Stronger than us, because she'd had to be;
Stronger than men. This proves the fallacy.
Her triumph, like her wealth, was all men's making,
And now she's in their funny cupboard world,
Upside down, her voice a box of holes,
Blue sparklers jammed in the hollow of her head,
While they charge round the room with guns and shrieking,
And swear they'd rather die than play with dolls.

ABOUT THE JEWS

(from the Russian of Boris Slutsky)

Jews don't plant wheat.
Jews trade in corner-shops.
Jews go bald earlier.
More Jews are thieves than cops.

Jews are adventurers,
No good at war.
Ivan fights in the trenches.
Abram minds the store.

I've heard it since my childhood
And soon I'll be decrepit.
Still I can't escape it:
The chant of 'Jews, Jews'.

I've never been in trade.
I've never stolen, once.
I carry this damned race
Inside like a disease.

The bullets didn't get me
Which only goes to prove
None of the Jews was shot.
They all came back alive.

1950

(from the Russian of Evgeny Rein)

The cable-car rises, a red-hot blaze, to the Sanatorium Frunze
(Named after Ordjonokidze), sends a mirror of light to the coast-road.
There's plenty of choice in the shops here—from eighths of litres to halves.
On your left, the Diplomat's Rest House. Journalists go straight ahead.
We're not far from Sochi. I'm seeing all this for the very first time.
Wearing my jersey-knit trunks with the sky-blue *Dynamo* band,
I lounge in the shade of a beach umbrella, or hurl myself through the frontline
Of the quarrelsome breakers pitched steadily over the sand
By some Lord of the median term, some Black Sea spirit,
Looking out of the depths at the twentieth-century's backside.
There's womanly flesh in abundance—milk, terracotta, chocolate,
But the tastiest colour by far is that of a dumpling, deep-fried.
Everything's fine and appalling, and something is almost made clear.
Around sunset, a sense of foreboding creeps out of the Caucasus.
Closing your eyes, you're alarmed when dull, reddish pimples appear
In the lids like an eczema-rash, or some kind of horrible pox.
Koba's sun is still high; over Moscow and Ritsa, its zenith.
This same mountain eagle sees all, his attention is double-bright.
Whatever you know, protect. Keep your head down. Cherish
Yourself like your sight.

HERE I AM

(from the Russian of Bella Akhmadulina)

Here I am at two in the afternoon,
Held up by the midwife like a trophy.
Lutes play over my head, fairy-wands
Tickle me. All my soul understands
Is a flood of golden colour; here I am
On a burning day the summer before the War,
Gazing around at the beautiful creation.
With lullabyes and Pushkin ('The Snowstorm'),
I get into the habit of being alive.
But here I am, ruined by war, alas,
Subject to Ufa's gloomy supervision.
Winter and hospital, how white they are!
I notice that I haven't died. Those called
Instead, are blurry faces in the clouds.
Here I am, brimming with eagerness,
Ugly, bluish, body just set free,
Alert to something tinier than a sound.
Not until later will I value this
Habit of hearing an eternal roll-call
Of nameless things in my name-giving soul.
Here I am, decked in purple, haughty,
Young and fat. But I have trained my mouth
To shape the smile of a poet before death.
There is a game between word and word
That's like the trembling between heart and heart.
The single obligation is to trace it
Flowingly, with a casual, careful art.
These words are bride and bridegroom. Here am I

Declaiming, chuckling like a village priest
Who prays the secret union will be blest.
That's why the good fairies scatter whispers
And laughter. I'm extraordinary, marked out
By my forehead, my singer's curving throat!
I love these marks of singularity.
My hand dashes off like a young hound
After her prey, bringing it to the ground.
Here I am. But my soul stops. I can't move.
I curse and cry. Let the page stay white!
Even though it was given me from above,
My task could not be honourably completed.
I bend my neck to the torment of a harness.
How others weave their words, I couldn't say.
I haven't got the nerve, the craftiness.
Leave me alone. A little person, twin
Of everyone alive, here I am
Dozing on the train, my nodding face
Homely against my bag. I've little fame,
Thank God, and no more fortune than my neighbour.
I'm with my weary fellow-citizens,
Flesh of their flesh. It's good. Last in the queue
That stretches endlessly from the cashier's
In shops, cinemas, stations, I'm the one
After the cheeky youth and the warm-shawled
Old woman, merging with them like a word
From my language and a word from theirs.

THE STONE BUTTERFLY

(for Kelsey & Rebecca)

Slow days, as a life prepares
To leave, discarding all
But its lightest necessaries.
Once we followed it
Through vivid stories, woven with our own.
We called it *Mum* or *Gran*, intimately.
Now, tired of our familiarity,
The life shifts, moves on
To a part we can barely read,
A hard, mysterious page, on which we glimpse
A figure so unselfconscious,
It could well be the long-ago child,
Scolded early to bed in her flowered nightdress.
The V-neck straggles across
The bare, innocent breast-bone,
The face, a kind of violence
To the face we expected, almost
As the child's must have been –
Flung open in grief or fury.
Fixed, now, beyond soothing.

But these are appearances, partial
Views from where we sit,
Tangled in life, still bound
By its tentative aesthetics.
The rich, layered protein bundle
Was meant to unfold, has always been unfolding.
When the molecules first talked and had ideas

That would be this particular person,
They allowed the heart a pause,
A moment's doubt for every great iamb,
And cells, already orphaned,
Were drifting from the untouched skin of the new.
The losses, heavier now,
May seem more soul-like:
A little blood that darkens
In the crook of the catheter,
Hunger, proprieties, the speakable words.
But this is her soul, too, this make-do-and-mend,
This Londoner's painful wit
That almost cheats each shortage
By a shrug, a *good riddance*,
And the sudden panic when
The black-out curtain slips.
Her hands fly into the night, then, signalling,
Lost and raw as fledglings tossed on a wind
To practise, until space
Becomes feathered, homelier.

That's when the slow day slows
Again, curves inwards.
We arrive again, and find
The curtains have closed ranks,
Broody as women in smocks
Waiting delayed appointments, the bare
Night-bulb burning as blue
As the dry blue dawn, and on other, less smooth pillows,
Eyes making out the grown-up shapes of day,
The dice swept back into the misty dream-cup.
She travels with quiet hands now,

And has taken only the smallest morning with her
For the sharp descent that cannot
Get easier.

But it does get easier:
The bundle almost peeled, only a little
Breath still saved in the lining,
To be spent in precise measures
Like childbed breath, but less,
Much less of it. And we must concentrate
On a new, exacter climb,
Feeling for toe-hold, stooping
Sometimes to pick up a keepsake,
Greedy now we know how small and cool
A hand becomes, a shell
Though we bind it, warm it, in our drowning fingers.

There will be harder things:
Keys that open wounds, rings to be counted,
Skins to be cast or worn.
Ghosts will leave dust or mist on the least expected
Surfaces: an envelope, which states
In familiar wobbly ovals
And swoops of cursive: *everything in order*.
And at once the bent white head and aching fingers
Will be an image I
Wipe off like tears, freeing
Something clear and achieved, its pride, its kindness:
The mind-thread glistening black
And alive as the veins on wings,
As if an envelope could be
That brilliant, weightless life she always wanted—
A butterfly. A manila butterfly.

For a time, we'll throw the dream-dice
And thoughts will flutter and play
Over a different horizon.
The world, we'll say, is sufficiently beyond us.
Rich postcards will arrive
From Eternity, a resort
Not yet built, but scripting its foundations
In super-matter, somewhere.
So we'll fly as far as we know
And come back sad, because gravity
Seems to own every airline,
And sit like children again
Being shown how to read
One more time, till slowly
Words become things, things become words, souls
And proteins pool their resources
And matter's highest kite—
Poetry, love, whatever—
Is tenderly reeled in through the dusk. Never mind.

Large-grained, each moment now
Widens, becomes a breath,
A sip of breath, brought
In a cup, by a machine,
But work for the whole feather-weight musculature,
The hand pulling from mine, a tiny pull,
As the lungs are forced to accept it
Again, again,
That punch of oxygen
Which starts the crying, rhymes the story on
And on, through chapters of plot

And counter-plot, into flashback
And metaphor, until wordless,
Hard-won, thread-like whispers are all that remains.

The day retreats a step.
The eyes close, choosing,
With sweet honesty,
To make it night. And still
An after-thought, an ellipsis,
The tongue in breath-space, trembling
As if it could offer us
A small 'and then'. And then
The forehead, huge and distant,
Suddenly whiter and, though quickly pressed
By lips, much farther away.

How can we say what happened? What we saw
Is all that can be said.
We can wish, of course, so fiercely
We nearly pray: that the body forgot to feel
How hard breath was, that the grace of all it had loved
Was received in every cell.

But for you and me, the end
Of the story is still guesswork,
And it's only my search for a not-unhappy full-stop
If I say how it seemed:
That something slipped very quietly
And unhesitatingly over

The edge of the day. It didn't
Flutter, fan itself up
To the lapis gates, the open halls of nectar
But fell like a stone, a fruit-stone, newly folded
To re-unfold, its contract with the earth
Binding as that of the sky-winged butterfly,
And death, no less than flight,
A natural miracle.

from **Holding Pattern** (1998)

ST. PETER'S WELCOMES THE PEACE WALKERS

Mini-skirted sixth-formers smile in the doorway,
Rattling donated boxes of Tunnock's Caramel Wafers.
Across the hall, their mothers and grandmothers
(The kind of women churchmen of all colours
Call 'our ministering angels') work with teapots.
The young priest welcomes the Methodists from the Shankill:
'We even painted the walls, look—just for you!'

I sit with two crisp-denimed Catholic women.
And soon we're friends, chatting about 'Queen's':
Maybe I've come across their student-children?
An older woman hovers, wants to join in
But won't sit down. She says she's not a marcher,
So it's not right: displays her ruined slippers.

'I'm on three types of pills,' she says, 'It's dreadful,
So it is. Abyssinia Street. A hell-hole.
D'you really like Belfast? Are you going to be staying?
I'm frightened to go out.'
'Couldn't you move,'
One of the women says kindly, 'to the suburbs?'

Something collapses in the long silence.
Call it religion. Say what emerges, naked
And guileless as the orange walls, is Class.

BOATING IN A BORDER COUNTY

Windless January dawn: the long rose-gold
Pulse across the tough so regular
It might have been an athlete's ECG.
The air glowed blue; even in the shed
Something filled the muddy pane like sky
Dreaming of itself.
                                        You said: 'Too heavy!'
'Och, no,' the owner said. 'But she wants cleaned.
She's not been touched the year.' You both kept on,
But I kept on against the two of you,
Woman enough, for once, to get my way.

The oars slither fractiously as you struggle
To get a grip, and then they're under orders,
The boat tastes open water, and we're moving
Sweet as a late quartet's deep-carved legato.
Your gaze relaxes past me into pleasure.
This is your art, reflexive as the waves,
And like an art ingrained the shore goes with us,
Shuffling contours, altering a tree line,
Losing one white farm, adding another,
But never past redemption, as we steer
Horizonwards, our quest, of course, an island.

Those distant, sombre, unrequiting islands!—
Mythic as winter wheat till we get near
And watch them fall apart like old rush-mats,
Such sloppy nests as wouldn't house a duck egg.
But when at last one offers foothold, homesick
Almost at once, we roam in circles, back

Through the thin coppice to our sidling craft
And there we broach the picnic like two babies,
Dandled, replete with liquidness and light.

We barely noticed, but a trail of mesh ,
A few splinter) stakes, have placed us south
Of where we woke, doubled our emigration.
I want to smile, imagining contraband
So simply shipped, but when I glance across
To see your happiness, that other border,
As vague, as definite, shivers between us:
The soul stain of your cancer diagnosis.

A turn so sharply wrong ruined our maps,
Roughed up our boat at first and nearly sank us.
Today, it marries us. The shudder passes,
And it's as if you've rowed us out to where
The future meets us, settling round our breath.
Enough, it sighs, enough!
Our precious future . . .
It was a form of childhood; we could leave it
On such a day, in such circumference.

Fermanagh, 1995

A DAY IN THE LIFE OF FARMER DREAM

In the morning light I stand outside my limits,
With equanimity survey the fields,
The thorn-hemmed acres that I call my land.
Some are ploughed, some newly sown, some thick
Already with astonishing wheat: some wait
Under a tat of kelp, or bask in clover.
In the morning light I lightly weigh my tasks:
A strong-jawed tractor stands on the hilltop,
The day burns to be off, time is enormous.
What happens in between I couldn't say,
But the grass has grown, and I return on foot,
A tinker or a tourist, one who gambled
Perhaps, or dawdled over skip and scrapyard,
Or slept because the blue was cradle-curved,
And ownership a gleam under a shawl.
Back west, the lying day projects its harvest
Of goldshine; dew is deepening round each stone,
And mist and I will climb the hill, soon, seeking
A house that wears the plume of our dissolving.

THIRST FOR GREEN

> *The trees are coming into leaf*
> *Like something almost being said . . .*
> PHILIP LARKIN
> 'The Trees'

Now their dreams are letting them through to the top of their wet
    black sleep
Though nothing has heard them stir yet. Only the hyacinths beading
The bed-fringe of each gaunt Kali, patient to match
Five o'clock's lavender cloud, and, along the square,
The lights coming on in the seminar rooms a little later each week
Seem to remember the trees will soon be awake.

It's easy to measure, still, the uneasy length of that street,
From the windows arched like prayers round the heavily pencilled
Shamrock and tudor rose, to the wish that, whatever occurred
In my chest, it was less like the trapdoor drop when the noose
Drags up a life in its fullness for the last breaking,
And hemp says to bone: your incident is closed.

If it had just been a season, a hibernation,
This grief-time, why is it growing, why is it rhyming with leaf-time?
There should be haulage and transport, the great distribution of sap
Flowing like silk through the restless loom of veins:
The story was written in water, I'd say, but listen, it rebegins
With a sigh from the root to the crown's wind-shaken, smoky tip.

But something as tight as despair winds round the throats of these
    thoughts.
Pathogens crowd where a thirst is disturbed by rain.
Is something wrong with the rain? It pales, refusing to climb

Towards the clamped buds in their dream of making light.
And then I remember: elms are cursed, spoor-thick with an old
disease.
And the spring crawls in like nothing on earth, with no leaf-
heraldries.

WORDS FOR POLITICIANS

The Party of Frogs is the Party of Toads
The Party of Comers, the Party of Roads
The Party of Gloves is the Party of Glands
The Party of Whispers, the Party of Bands
The Party of God is the Party of Good
If you haven't learnt that yet, you bloody well should

'Cos the Baseball-Bat Party's the Party for Learning
The Book Party's party to Naughty-Book Burning
The Bring-Back-the-Past Party's fighting for Progress
The Yes-No Brigade utters nothing but No-Yes
The Green Party's Pink and the Can Party Couldn't
And if you believe me you bloody well shouldn't

'Cos Doubt is the Party of Bold Self-Assertion
The Party of Faith is the Party-Sized Version
The Idiots' Party's the Party for Smarties
The Party from Hell is the Party of Parties
The Party for Fish is the Party for Bait
And you'd swallow anything, wouldn't you, mate

'Cos the Anything Party's the Party of Sellers
The Bendy Spoon Party's that Party of Geller's
The Party of Saddam's the Party of Freedom
The Party of Women is out – we don't need 'em
The Party of Lagan's the Party of Boyne
And if you don't like it you still have to join

'Cos the Party of Like-It's the Party of Lump-It
The Party of Muffin's the Party of Crumpet

The Bakery Party's the Party of Ormeau
The Sunny Twelfth Party's the Party of Lawn-Mow
The Party of Nine is the Party of Six
If not then there's nothing a penknife can't fix

'Cos the Party of Cut is the Party of Run
The Popular Front is a Party of One
The Smoke-Alarm Party's the Party of Fags
The Party of Gays is the Party that Drags
The PUP is a Party no doggie wants in
If you start a New Party don't think it will win

'Cos the Fresh Approach Party's the Party of Same
The Alzheimer's Party's forgotten its name
The Residents' Party arrives by the coachload
The Pesticide Party is really a Roachload
The Party of Bread's on the Party of Shelves
If you want some more Parties, twist words for yourselves.

WHERE THE RAINBOW ENDS

Halfway down Cranmore Park, it becomes dear
 That the road is heading straight for the roots of the hills:
The trees descend like a wavy slide at a fair:
 The city's abandoned, green will flourish for miles.

Up go the hills to heaven, as sinlessly
 As pets, with their velvet flanks, their stripes and tufts,
And down, down slips the road, black gravity
 Tarring my feet while my gaze, free-floating, lifts.

The trees soon tire of the game. They block the way
 Scots pines, chestnuts, larches – glorious things
But proud and a little cold, inclined to weigh
 And sift their shade above fussy gardenings.

And then there are so many chimneys saluting the sky
 Their fists have all but obliterated the blue
Not to speak of the green, which looked so near, so true,
 But now seems merely the memory of a trompe l'œil.

Mourn as I might, I haven't any choice
 But to turn my rise to my fall, and let the hills
Dissolve, as a face dissolves into a house,
 Leaving the stranger nothing but roads and rules.

INEDUCABLE

Looking out on that drenched street my heart
half-listening as I say not this again
it echoes *this again* and I continue
to look half-seeing am I not alive
to all rain does to stone isn't my passion
for being free for being sensible
to all rain does to stone isn't my passion
to look half-seeing am I not alive
it echoes *this again* and I continue
half-listening as I say not this again
looking out on that drenched street my heart

CONVERSATION WITH A SEAGULL

(in memoriam Joseph Brodsky)

Poem-maker, your guild disbanded, not one
  Man left at his station:
Love-adept, at last unbefriended, no-win
  Your situation,
So what if some cloud from your most Aquarian mood,
  Or a snowflake of brain,
Drift above Shandon, prospecting for Leningrad
  Through thickening rain,
Puzzling in vain for the wobbly Venetian Os
  Of arch-backed embraces,
The aristocratic self-disregard of *palazzos*?
  Such weathers aren't voices.
Say the feathery soul of your river-love just gave a cry
  As it dived from the railing—
A gull is a Soviet type, mass-produced, sly.
  Your wings would be flailing.
Whether nature plays God is still what I want to know.
  Can selves be re-formed
Like the river from rain? And now I can hear it—abseiling
  In spirals down from your vast oratorical
Rucksack—the question. *The question, Kerol*, you're saying,
  Is surely rhetorical?
The self is—well—imaginary, and it will go
  Nowhere—or wherever imaginings go.

Cork, 1996

TO POETRY

My darkest eye, the one I've never seen
In any glass, changes the day with you,
Colouring bridally, though out of season,
Like hills in sudden scarves of frost or bracken.
It knows your fiercest winter hex, but stays
Patient, snow-lidded, meeting dark with dark.
It loves the rose-bright pulse of you in health:
Its vein runs to your heart, picks up the song.
It sees you best when everyday eyes sleep,
But should these daily eyes lose sight of you
The meanest light will never meet my road.

STANZAS FOR A NEW START

Home for a long time fought with me for air,
And I pronounced it uninhabitable.
Then, in an old tradition of reversal,
I understood I'd left my future there.

I chased across the badlands of recession:
I'd make a bid for any cuckoo's nest
That sang the joys of owner-occupation.
No loan shark lacked the details of my quest.

Now it's acquired refinement. It's a passion
Long-pursued, a serious late career.
I've shelved my dreams of contract and completion.
Haste doesn't suit the eternal first-time buyer.

Home, after all, is not a simple thing.
Even indoors there should be garden voices,
Earth-breaking rootage, brilliant mirroring,
A constant foliation of loved faces.

Doors are a must, but let them make a palace,
Let each room smile another, on and on—
The glittering, the plain, the small, the spacious,
The sacred and the haunted and the one

Hope rests her case in—windswept, cornerless.

from **Hex** (2002)

DECEMBER TENNIS

Winter's first ice!
Green pavings of it, smashed
and sealed on the little lake. No swans,
mallards, kids—only an old ribbed dustbin
rolled on its side like the park drunk on his seat.

To make you growl
Carol, Carol,
I volunteer a toe
and up comes bold black jack-in-the-box, oh
wicked, delicious, soaking one new Nike.

We're for the courts.
Is it Lux or Dreft
they're powdered with? Such velvet
beneath our heels of sky!

Play is the rosebud gift
we gather yet.
Our old wood low-tech racquets
can flash, trampoline, taking
bows when we're in our stride—although
my first shot slugs the net—too low.

There's a circle in Hell
for love like ours. But the ball
survives the serve, the beautiful curve of our planet
reels from our palms, and the sun,
a toe-dipping god, is splashing the trees and the fence
across our dance in huge harmless meshed
Xs and Ys!

KINGS OF THE PLAYGROUND

All to get the Bully—who hid in a steel-clad cupboard—
the Bully Bashers stormed the trembling school.
They bullied the Bully's kit, his grubby blazer,
his sports-bag, his bully-beef flavour crisps.

They bullied the kids with the bruises
that showed the Bully's shoe-print.
They bullied the gerbils he'd teased, they bullied every computer
he'd slimed with his bully virus.

They bullied the prefects and teachers—
the nice ones first then the bullies.
The kids who had conduct stars, the kids in detention, even
the football team, they bullied, yelling 'Ya bullying fairies!'

They bullied the books, though the Bully didn't like books:
they bullied the white-boards and black-boards,
they bullied the wall-charts, the registers, the sick-notes,
the pass-notes. They bullied the two-times table.

Then they thundered out and bullied the empty playground,
they bullied the big round sky that covered the playground,
they bullied the rain, the bushes, the used needles,
the trembling waiting parents, the tiny brothers and sisters.

Bully TV was launched. There was only one programme
'How We Bashed the Bully'. Anyone who switched off
was sentenced to 25 years community-bullying.
The Bully-Bashers relaxed. Gave themselves medals. Flew home.

The Bully listened a while, and grinned in the dark cupboard.
He combed his hair. He opened the door wide.
He sauntered through the wrecked assembly hall.
Scared faces turned. Eyes that remembered his bruises

clouded over, younger eyes grew shiny.
Suddenly someone shouted, 'Look, the Bully!
Them liars didn't get him! Three cheers for our Bully!'
And everyone yelled and stamped: 'Three cheers for old Bully!'

Old Bully mounted the stage. How tall he was,
what a lovely speech he made. The big boys lifted him high
and they all stormed into the trembling streets, yelling
'Make way for Old Bully, ya cunts!' And the people did.

SHADE

might seem pure negative. But do you remember
when it was solid, delicious as a late breakfast?
We'd been in the fields since 6 a.m., training
the new kiwi-plants to weave thick cool tunnels
for next season's pickers, stringing the wayward tendrils
to the trellises that would lead them up and over.
There were few leaves on those apprentice vines,
nothing to beat back the power of the sky.
We watched our forearms shrivel like eggs in a pan.
What amateurs of the sun, what holy fools
we were, out there in the desert in our tee-shirts,
as if a god would pity human skin.

At noon the day was over, called off.
We crossed the fields to the avocado orchards
where we flung ourselves down, the team of us, speechless.
The cool-box broached, we dived into whole grapefruit.
Can you remember what the word *shade* meant there?
How we pulled it on, over our scalps and eyes,
and it was the end of all headaches,
how we rinsed our faces in it again and again,
how we buried ourselves in its arms and heard our names?
If death were to be like this, would we call it loss?
We'd know, long before we were cold, that a great wish had been
granted.

DROPLETS

Tiniest somersaulter
through unroofed centuries,
puzzling your hooped knees
as you helter-skelter,
dreamy, careless,
without a safety net
into an almost-ness
as uneventfully lost,
your house re-let,
guiltless defaulter:

sex: un-noted: weight:
a minimal gravity:
whatever you'd have tried
in time amounting to,
unguessed, undone—
I'd have your cry
brought home—and yet
when you demand to live,
these hands that blessed
your hopeful forehead, answer
only in negative.

RIGOR MORTIS

Someone should tell them they're dead.
Two rigid soldiers
are facing across a bridge,
facing at point-blank range:

two rigid soldiers,
both men ready to fire,
facing at point-blank range
the shot that stops the war,

both men ready to fire,
when the starter signals,
the shot that stops the war
of two land-eating lands.

When the starter signals,
watched by the empty children
of two land-eating lands,
they fire at each other's frowns.

Watched by the empty children
at either end of the bridge,
they fire at each other's frowns,
two soldiers, sights refocused

at either end of the bridge.
It's like science fiction:
two soldiers, sights refocused,
swallowing shot like bread.

It’s like science fiction.
This can’t be ordinary flesh
swallowing shot like bread,
and poised to fire again.

This can’t be ordinary flesh,
its weaponry always loaded
and poised to fire again.
Two bundles of riddled land

in a carcass of battle-dress
are facing across a bridge
they think is worth dying for.
Someone should tell them they’re dead.

RELIGIOUS EDUCATION

The god of human love was king of kings,
Then, to our wooden classroom: where a child's
Finger moved, a small star cruised above it,
Nervously eyeing shapes beyond the wind.
I could dim any light and see it now,
The silver-on-black word, *epiphany*,
And find, brimming my hands, the charged rewards
For having, being, nothing. Is there mercy
In any universe for us, who knelt
Crownless among the hungry, kicking lambs,
And touched the star, we numerous underlings
Who now believe in all kinds of imaginary things?

EICHMANN IN MINSK

> *As I arrived I saw a Jewish woman with a small child in her arms in the pit. I wanted to pull the child out, but then the bullet hit the child's head. I got back into the car. 'Berlin,' I said to my driver. I drank Schnapps as if it was water. I had to dull my brain.*
> THE DIARIES OF ADOLF EICHMANN

Drinking *Schnapps like water,* stare
Until the moment's hardly there,
Until the shapes in the forest's floor
Stiffen, fade and rise no more
As limbs and mouths with claims to air,

And trees fly back to the clearing where
The bony-shouldered spades prepare
To meet the load from the lorry door,
On schedule, as you'd planned before
Drinking Schnapps like water.

Nothing's there! So grown-ups swear.
So history lies. So bodies bear
The heavy measures ordered for
Disposal. It is only your
Child you pity, almost spare,
    Drinking Schnapps like water.

FALLING MAN

From another angle,
it's as if the lens
had caught him asleep,
dawn-lit, gripped
by one of those vivid
pre-waking bad
dreams, where the brain
e-mails itself:
this isn't happening.
Not the illusion
of stillness, but
the lack of distortion,
casualness, almost,
in his posture, his body's
so-far unflawed
completeness, muddles
our narrative grasp.
He can handle this.
It's only air,
air that was always
our element, made
to breathe and burn,
to be built into,
and risen above,
the trespass-inviting
pitch whose one
amazing floodlight
names us co-stars.

We had to look up:
we bathed our eyes
in light so they learned

colour, stretched arms
and lungs into Os
of desire: we found
trees to feed us,
mountains to teach us,
like sleepers waking,
kept ascending,
poised on the tip
of our soaring backbone
until there was less
and less air: maladapted,
enchanted, we still
saw ways to increase
height, flung up towers,
flew fortresses, looped
skyway to skyway:
we 'conquered space'
as we phrased it, trawling
our own supplies
of oxygen, rushed
up, floated down,
not quite admitting
what thrust had been required,
suspecting we'd grown
at least one small wing.

But the love of surface
stuck to our soles.
And our sun-gods, turning
to stone, sang out
from their beautiful hardness:
dive, plunge,
be scattered over

your disputed cities
and shine beyond memory!
Gods need our trust:
then they'll catch the shadow
of a man, falling,
or a man, flying
into his future,
who smiles as it stops
and spins him a tunnel
in which he hangs
as others are hanging
outside their windows
and walls like pupas
waiting to split
into moths, new man-moths,
and fly away, lighter
than poetry.

The steeper the fall,
the wilder the angle
of rebound: this
is emotional physics.
We sting as we die,
like ants, we roll
our alchemical dead
into thunderheads, gather
as balled-up stars
and pelt the world
with skull-bits, billions
of crumbled backbones
to feed the soil,
to grow the new tall.

From the air, nothing hurts.
The air itself
is nursery blue
and safe as steel—
threaded towers. And our hands
move over the face
of the deep, they are all—
powerful: look,
they can dump fire
on selected targets
while turning a page
horizontally,
to pause this diver,
laying him safely
on Slumberland foam,
him and his heart-plunging
nightmare, his billowing
shirt, his scream
fading to daybreak's
patter of shower-tiles,
running-shoes, pavement—
the usual welcome
of nearby earth,
G-forces impalpable
now to one quick,
finely-braced ankle,
one kicked-back heel.

THE 'PASTIME' SCHOOL OF POETS

Poems I might have written for my father,
had he lived long enough, had I learned quicker
to find the vital signs inside the daft
corseted minuets and crumbly sword-play
of borrowed language: had I not ranged against him
my revolution, where a poem was measured
beside the shapes of things just made, lit blocks
I loved, wrought in Black Mountain foundries or
night-brilliant power stations in the depths
of Europe—poems my father couldn't see
at all, and wouldn't touch because they'd burn
harsh chemical shadows, blanching rays
into the poems he loved, the lines he whispered
to make them breathe and enter, turn, and echo
through courteous archways, genuflecting slightly
towards that dangerous place, the margin: poems,
once gifts, now telling him he had no gift,
a man who scribbled 'poems' as a pastime,
a man who *scribbled*: —poems be crushed in bins
or ashtrays, draw their smoke, flatten their crinkled
surfaces and flow across my keyboard
as poems I might have written for my father
for him to love, and to be loved by others;
I stand back as they pass, admiring how
simply they press towards their vanished moment,
freed from gentility, made truthful by
the silence darkening round them, as I once
darkened my poor father with my silence:

poems too late for giving, poems that whisper
if poems don't hurt us, are they truly poems?
but claim no power to burn, are almost weightless
among the graves of books and revolutions
and old beliefs that such things are immortal:
poems I'll write for no one, for a pastime.

THE ARRIVAL

There are days early in love when love knows nothing
but to exist between our thoughts, unremarkable, vaguely
grand—as the future did when we were children.
Nothing becomes love more than when he dozes
like this, a jet-lagged wanderer, curled over his wallet,
his possibly false papers. *I'm the one:*
arrest me! is the last thing he would say.

THE SUBMERGED CATHEDRAL

(in memory of Phyllis Robinson)

> *I have made mysterious my religion . . . to feel the*
> *supreme and moving beauty of the spectacle to which Nature*
> *invites her ephemeral guests, that is what I call prayer.*
> Claude Debussy

It's an hour before the dawn of rock 'n' roll:
Music has not so far been made flesh—
Or nor for a working-class girl of thirteen.
And then I watch you play, star graduate
Of James Ching and the Matthay School,
Your technique so physical, so lavish,
I'd call it, now, *l'ecriture feminine*
For pianists: but in 1958
All I know is that you are what you're playing—
You're playing *La Cathédrale Engloutie*.

A camera's drawn to the concert pianist's hands,
Caressing octaves, palely capering—
Sunday *Palladium* stuff, with Russ Conway
Or Winifred Atwell (coos from the mums and dads),
To be filed under my new word: *Philistine*.
This is art so deep it's industry:
Music as white-water, which your spine
Channels, springing arms transform. That's how
You lift and tumble these ton-weights of bell power:
I watch you, not your hands. I watch the sea,

Out of my depth, though, like *La Cathédrale*.
I mean all this to last—the eight hours' practice
Each day, hopeless devotion—and it does—
In other contexts. Oh, I bury it,

Music, and you, and all the pain of childhood,
But lumber back like a medieval builder
With washed-up stones (some good stone, too) and prayers,
To raise another heaven-touching marvel
On the same flood-site, watch another tide
Swagger in and demolish every bit.

After the last wreck, when I'd declared
The end of building-works on any coast,
Strange bells began to ring for me, the tone
Rubbed ordinary by forty years, but true:
Ghostly but not damned. What if the ghost
Wryly sang, 'Promises, promises?'
It was a gentle challenge, after all.
The sacred stones were myth. The tide that reared
So vengefully, hauled by the same moon,
Was myth. Not so, my common ground with you.

How we talk up 'the generation gap',
Break our necks in it, and never find
The friendly criss-cross trails of co-existence—
That gift which is to pause at one epoch,
The people of one earth. Yes, the years wear us . . .
But may all years be worn as you wore yours
That day we met, with teacherly compassion,
Because the body knows when the brighter mind
Rejects it, sulks like an untuned piano:
You lived in yours (it knew) like the luckiest girls.

It's hard, though, for the tired cells to sightread
Their last prélude, fingers twisting palm-ward,
In search of rarer ivory, their guiding
Beat a laggard stone-deaf walking-stick.
Like Schubert's songs, off in another key
Before we can say 'swan', you were elsewhere:
And elsewhere, in a room nearby, your music.
I'd wanted you to play. I let that go.
You counted off your new pursuits, confiding
'I love the sea. I love to watch *la mer*!'

On Portrush Strand I watch it too, engrossed
Like a child beside a piano, half aware
That this, whatever 'this' may be, won't keep,
The waves themselves won't keep. But someone plays
Debussy. Something rescues the white horses
You're not admiring now – not from these shores,
And makes them flesh, as music was, for me,
An hour before the dawn of rock 'n' roll
When you, star graduate of the Matthay school,
Lifted the great bells out of the sea.

AGAINST POSTERITY

Gather round me now, you older poets—
Poets in your late forties, early fifties,
Mid-fifties—you who understand
The significance of these small demarcations:
Poets of three-score years and pension book,
Superbly unretiring, with or without a *festschrift*
Made by the admirers you'll never become:
Poets triumphant in your racy seventies,
And you, especially you, in your eighties and nineties,
Maire, Dasenka, Kathleen—marvellous sisterhood—
Bring your short breath and your dancing stanzas.
And don't be shy, you grandfathers and great-grandfathers,
Though poems may be your only progeny—
Hey, you with the tinsel beard, no bardish pride!
This is a call for solidarity
Surpassing miserly gender (oh, forget about gender:
By now it's surely forgotten about us).
Spread the news of your brilliant forthcoming collection,
The Whitbread and the Forward in the bag,
But raise a not unkindly eyebrow at
The Gregory girls and boys still trembling at first base.
Tell us your publishers love you more and more,
But if you've travelled the hard road from nowhere
To sunny fame then down to the council tip
Of the out-of-date, declare with modest humour
The world has yet to match your three-legged stride
Along the crest of that hill it hasn't noticed yet.
Be tacit, but imply you won't go gentle

Like clowning Dylan, nor in Plath's hard rage,
To freeze with those who would have graced our gathering
With wit and beauty and magnificence
Had they cherished themselves as they cherished language.
Poetry's for grownups. So gather round, who know
Their music isn't the new rock 'n' roll
But a late quartet that sometimes bursts out laughing.
Bring your sustaining harmonies, let rip with your solos,
Unfurl surprises till the final chord,
When we'll forgive your silence—as ours will be forgiven—
And make way a little grudgingly
For the new recruits, who'll seem a shade too youthful.

ANYTHING/NOTHING

He becomes lame
    she stops
        climbing mountains

he loses some of his hearing
    she loses
        some of her tongue

he forgets to admire her body
    she ceases to admire
        any body

young marriage doubles the joy
    old marriage halves it

    and so she begins
paring lengths from his sight

    but remembers to shout
a joke in his best ear
    clink of glasses

    they share the mountain
at the kitchen window
    determined to savour

    seagull, sheep, stone
he names the snowdrifts for her
    the half-measure

oh how they work to keep
this earth that's so much harder
so much bigger, now,

than anything
than nothing

TO THE SHIPBUILDER, HIS TABERNACLE

Leave the shed-door open:
It's all that lights the garden once we've crossed
Your solstice-shaded birthday.
Dusty martyrs' crowns on the young ivy
Are the best we can do for autumn flowers:
Our rooftop-transept banishes the sunbeds
To Evensong by four.
But this door has a forest's eyes; when cedar
Bristles back to its origins, the day
Sticks like honey, never wants to let go.

Did we know we were buying sunlight,
Driving out to one of those desolate
Life-style hangers on the edge of town,
Strolling the wooden shtetl?
It was your birthday. I was feeling rich.
As if I'd been stockpiling English dreams
For the first Ukrainian-Jewish-Russian-Finn
Who'd crossed the border into B and Q
I wrote a cheque to make the best and dearest
More yours than Moscow.

You got inside at once, opening crystals
Of space with a submariner's
Eye for horizons, deep in stacking-systems.
Tools lined the decks like sailors,
Some bright, some sleepy. Rusty captains stowed
Their wooden legs upright. Tins on tins,

Labelled *almond cake, pitted olives, ikra*
Rattled with machine-food.
You pinched the nameplate from your office door
When they 'retired' you, fixed it to the shed.

And if the wood by now
Is being turned by micro-organisms,
Glued with a frost of cobwebs,
The gentle molecules of oil and creosote
Tired of stretching: if I submit and say
That autumn's pollen, halo-ing the ivy,
Was gold enough, more than we could have asked for,
Don't go before I've told you, with a wife's sad humour—
Leave the shed door open
So that I'll sometimes see you.

WOOD LOVERS

And a time will come when we drive on, ignoring
The grassy welcome-mat outside the pine trees' barracks
And our infallible instinct to surprise
Some tiny village, light-forgotten, stained
Cupolas lined with pleated pearl and coral.
And a time will come when our legs refuse to vanish
Far enough to uncloud the bluebell islands,
Or the windflower archipelago, white as Sweden:
And then a time when there's no wood, no forest,
No signposts for the words that keep on saying your voice:
Griboclzki, kolokolclziki, clwroshi less.

REFRESHER COURSE

Drifting at dawn out of staticky hurricane dreams
to the clearest blue ever sieved through a wet tent wall,
to the shock of grass in its first-day sky, and the roar
of the river-beast, the whole sheep orchestra
sending each other a wobbly, hopeful 'A'
and never needing to reach the symphony,
we knew we had altered time. Time was our child
like the child of old parents, a huge reach
encompassed: we would shed years every day.

In or out of the tent, time flew: we caught it
occasionally, we gave it different nicknames,
to do with light. The only tune it knew
was *Variations of a Theme of Rain*:
gas-rings and rain, dishes and soap and rain,
blankets beginning to steam and sparkle; rain,
wood-fires spitting at rain, wine with a spritz of rain:
rain in the bones, pricking, darning, tugging.
Once, playing *Hunt the Sun,* it let us win:
we stood at the wet kissing-gate and felt
the brush of dim warm animals called rainbow.

Imagine a life as just-made glass, so clean
it was invisible, self-polishing.
It never asked us to notice it until
the leaving day. Stroke after stroke appeared
and wrote: *we were happy here*. And happiness paid
its last pound-coin to the casual farmer.
Our feet crept home as shoes, our wrists as sodden
watch-strap; we could see the day was filthy,

and time, drumming enormous adult heels,
hated our straw house, our joke umbrellas.
We talked about going back, perhaps next week.
But only one of us did. And only like this.

SWEDISH EXCHANGE

When we entered the room it was white. The lampshade was blue, circular, patterned with circular holes. A white half-curtain at the window was printed with ellipses of different colours. There was a flat mirror in a wooden frame that was curved, lending the glass a faint concavity. A whitewood table and two chairs. A red mat.

We made the red mat dirty. On the table we put a glass of lilies of-the-valley: they had cost thirty kroner on a street corner somewhere near the Klara church. The woman who sold them said: you must give them cold water! There is a blue dictionary on the table containing 30,000 *ord och fraser* and, on the window-sill, a lime-green tennis-ball containing a finite but unknown number of bounces. The mirror is full of badly hung clothes. Light sometimes leaks from the lamp-shade holes, the chairs refuse to sit at the table.

To make the room simple again we will have to leave it. We ourselves will have to re-complicate. This is a pity. We'd like to leave the room not as we found it but as we made it, impressed with our favourite transfers. The room would be grateful. And we would be white, clean, with natural wood features and a few splashes of primary colour, an excellent design for the modern human. We would close the door and not invite ourselves back in.

QUOTATIONS

What I like about quotations
is their loneliness

what I like about loneliness
is seven and a half vodkas-and-blackcurrant

what I like about blackcurrants
are the sharp little stones inside their burst cushions

what I like about cushions
is their lack of backbone

what I like about the backbone
is its perfection

what I like about perfection
is academic

what I like about academics
is the way they curl two fingers when citing quotations

(Etc.)

LEARNER

She tried to make a life out of dead things:
A woman's gravestone eyes, a man's drowned smile.
With all her breath, muscle, cherishings,
She tried to make a life. Out of dead things
False life alone can come, but since 'hope springs'
Et cetera, for a long laborious while
She tried to make a life out of dead things.

A woman's gravestone eyes a man's drowned smile.

LETTER

(i.m.Yehuda Amichai)

Love is not, you told us, the last room
In the long corridor that has no end.
Young till that moment, I had not imagined
Rooms beyond love—not rooms with life in them,
But now I felt a season of decorum
Cooling my breeze. I thought I too could rise,
Brush off my suitors, seek those ghostly floors
Most distant from the heart and the heart's heat.
Reaching at last the *sanctum sanctorum*,
I'd notice further doors, hemmed with faint rays
(The corridor was long, you said, was endless),
Find rooms it seemed too soon to talk about
While time could laugh. Clutching your groundplan, still
Convinced, I came of age. And here I've learned
That the heart's room, as well, may have no end.
Windows may seal and fade, and doors unhandle,
Lit outlines melting into wall-thick mist.
Wherever you are now, in rooms beyond
My grasp, I write to say—it would appear
That the first room, love's, may also be the last
Though love is now an absence, cornered there.

THE FITTING ROOM

I was a legend in my mother's lifetime
And marvelled as the name I never took
Did cute or comic things in simple rhyme
Or dazzled like an easy-reading book.
'But I grew up,' I said. 'What happened after?'
She didn't know. Perhaps her heart intoned,
'They are not long, the weeping and the laughter,'
But, terrified to entertain such thoughts,
She went on joining up the dot-to-dots,
And, at her side, the child of fifty groaned.

I had no life to share, few words to say,
Till she lay dying. Then, the legend spoke,
Spoke legends in the colours she'd have chosen,
I hoped, to warm a cave untouched by day.
Words failed her, but her mouth, crookedly open,
Seemed to be laughing at the little joke
Death makes of life. Since then, I've found a tongue
Too quick, I think, at argument and blame,
And yet I've half a hope she sits among
My readers—those who know my grown-up name.

She'll tell the tale that fits like me like a glove
And I won't feel diminished, saying Mother,
Mummy, Mum. Why is so much of love
The kind of gift you know was made by hand
And not made well, some weird, tenderly-knit
Garment that doesn't suit, won't ever fit?
I'll guess it was her love I called a legend.
I thought it shrank me, sought an ampler space.
But she's the legend now—the way I tell her,
My funny gift. My loss. My crooked face.

AUTUMN COLOURS

High overr Petersburg, gold and red
Like a Khokhloma soup-spoon, a kitchen gleams
And mists with fragrance, just as it did
When you were the boy with the bowl of dreams.
But the grown-ups died and the tall young man
With the lacquered money and laughing wife,
Can't be the one who fills the word, *son*:
As he shakes your hand he unmakes your life,
  Saying 'Pack up your troubles, Pa, let's go
  To the Fountain of Youth or some place you know.
  The fountain's fucked and the weeds smell vile
  But the fags are cheap, so smile, boys, smile.'

And you picture the banners, red and gold,
And all they meant or should have meant:
They've gone with the gods and the country, sold
For a song whose words aren't any you learnt
As a Young Pioneer. You can move as you please
But the town on your papers isn't your town.
Each rolling Mercedes is full of old faces
Same apparatchik, faster gun.
  Then pick up your kit, that place is scary.
  Better retire to Tipperary.
  It's a long long way, as the war-vets sing
  But nearer, my love, than your Leningrad spring.

ROGUE TRANSLATIONS

1 Once

(After 'Ya Vas Lubil' by ALEXANDER PUSHKIN*)*

I loved you once. D'you hear a small '*I love you*'
   Each time we're forced to meet? Don't groan, don't hide!
A damaged tree can live without a bud:
   No one need break the branches and uncover
The green that should have danced, dying inside.
   I loved you, knowing I'd never be your lover.
And now? I wish you summers of leaf-shine
   And leaf-shade, and a face in dreams above you,
   As tender and as innocent as mine.

2 Special Exhibition

(After 'Mirskaya Vlast' by ALEXANDER PUSHKIN*)*

A craftsman made an image of a crucified god.
His prayer, in time, became a work of art
And stood in a museum under armed guard.
2000 years ago, the original prophet,
A mystery to us now, hung slowly dying,
Dying, as he'd lived, among the undeserving poor,
Flanked by thieves, his cherished women crying -
One said to be a virgin, one, a whore.
Now, where they leant, impassive policemen reign,
And no one else gets near the exhibit.
Wannabes watch and pray and sip champagne,
The star's not here. He couldn't afford the ticket.

3 *We'll Meet Again*

(After ' *V Peterburge mie soidyomsya snova' by* Osip Mandelstam.
The speaker is a South Londoner of the early 1940s.)

We'll meet again in 'Peter'.
We'll dig up that Victory sun
and say the word again—
our blessed, daft little word.
The Soviet night's a nag called Black Velvet.
The empty universe is a pint of Black Velvet.
We'll bet on the empty universe.
Long as our favourites are on-stage, our troupers
who never say die—long as you never say die, girls—
we'll all come up roses.

Like a cornered moggie, the town
whips up a humpback bridge complete with sentry.
A wicked car rips solo through the gloom—
cuckoo, cuckoo.
I don't need your old pass, ta very muchly.
You can tell the guard where to get off.
Give me crimson velvet, a couple of tickets,
that hush, that nervous rustling,
silky as silk stockings.
A girl cries 'whoops' and Venus takes a bow,
up to her cherries in roses.
I'm praying to you, little word. My daft little wonderful word.
Boredom stares at the gas-fire, roasting its knees.
Was that the sandman passing,
leaving a smear of ash
on the arms we knew and blessed?

Those crimson curtains, deep as orchestras,
Those treasure-boxes, stuffed
like gran's chiffonier
with clockwork captains and their china dolls—
bastards and hypocrites haven't got an inkling!
Put out the candles, son, if that's the boss's orders.
Put up the old black cretonne. The women'll just shrug
their luscious shoulders, won't you, girls, and keep
right on singing. Bless you.

Singing shoulders, blooming banks of roses,
the sun lit up all night—and you never saw sweet FA!

4 *The Grape-picker*

(After Fasti. III. Non. 5th, by Ovid)

By the fifth morning, when the dew has dried
  On the saffron cheek of Tithonus' wife, Aurora,
Instead of the Great Bear and the sleepy Herdsman,
  You'll see the Grape-Picker, curly-haired Ampelus,
Stretch out his boyish hand. This is his story:
  Child of nymph and satyr, he was playing
Among the Ismanian hills one day when Bacchus,
  Idly watching, fell for him utterly.
And he sang up a drunken gift, an enormous vine, fruit-laden,
  And trailed it over the highest bough of an elm tree.
Scrambling along to reach the glowing clusters,
  Ampelus lost his balance, pitched over headfirst.
Bacchus lifted the small corpse from the hillside.
  He placed it in a canopy of swaying, grape-bright stars.

5 The Things He Liked

(After 'On liubil tri veshi na svet' by ANNA AKHMATOVA*)*

He liked secret agents, submarines.
He had a soft spot for the Thames Barrier.
And he was tied to me.

He read big books from remainder shops,
All about *things*, the things
He liked: secret agents, submarines,

Our Mysterious Universe,
The Volvo 300 Series,
And he was tied to me

Who couldn't read a fuel-gauge.
He hated long talks about feelings.
He liked secret agents. Submarines

Were a primitive fascination.
They were his youth, his memory,
And he was tied. To me

He was Naval Intelligence. I kept bugging him.
I stroked his prow, promised to play at whatever
He liked: *secret agents, submarines*,
And he was tied to me.

from **New Poems** (2004)

TO SAVE THE WHEEL

(after Highways and Byways *by Paul Klee)*

But the byways also took us
  to our only feasible
    horizon.

We hadn't got lost, turned
  at too sharp an angle:
    it was our road, we pressed

on homelessly, vaguely,
  to the blue,
    to the fire-face,

peeling off minerals, mammals,
  stripping and grafting,
    the only way we knew

to save the wheel,
  and the road that re-invents it—
    the wheel and everything.

THE BALTIC SWAN

Steadily striving inland,
Until so close it was in the realm of the personal,
And we called it 'he', after *lebed*,
(Masculine, Russian), the single Baltic swan
Had the dangerous shape of two contrary instincts,
Hunger and fear. And, though hunger drove him,
His wide and zigzag course, the wind-defying
Braced flare of his archangel, Aztec wings
Signalled the cross he carried.

How dearly he wanted not to give up the sea,
But he'd sighted (scented, heard, felt in the tides
Around him, in him?) something
Half-learnt far back—a featherless ideogram
That pictured *Eat! Survive!*
And we, who spelled so much, watched and were gripped
By his translation. He was like the island;
He was its language, *Nature*: big clean words
Knotted in our own wrack, if we could only find them.

On foot, he at once lost style.
He wobbled, lurched, his splayed
Froggy webs and fine shins overloaded
With gravity, the sheer dry weight of him.
But he wasn't turning back. He aimed straight at us,
Huge shields ablaze. The almost comical
Face-mask—Loyalist-orange, ebony-trim—
Fixed just beneath his eyes,
Shocked us like a drawn gun: pure swan,
As guns are pure man, his diamond essence.

We tried not to gasp, we couldn't speak
As he squashed himself onto our picnic rock,
A swan eclipse, spilling all over the inch
He'd put between his tottery world and ours.

He rolled a little, like a sea-filled barrel,
Snorted, preened his foam,
Then leaned from the fleece-packed muscle of his neck
And probed the safest, nether bits of us—
Bottles, wrappers, my discarded sandals.
He tried my toes for texture, delicately.
I breathed my pulse to normal.
Showing fear was out: we'd refuse that exchange.
(Weren't we the brains here?) Slower than slow motion
One of us picked the loaf up, tore
Some small, sweet pieces, and we flattened
Our palms to bony plates, to say we meant
All the good he wanted (Eat! Survive!)—
And laid it out for him, our only meaning.

The neck dipped, the horn spoon poked and scooped.
We tore fresh pieces, ate our own scant share
Until the loaf ran out,
And we folded up our hands to show goodbye,
He snapped once at my sandal, and agreed,
Dragged himself to his feet, swayed back to the water.
He faded slowly, lingering at the margin,
Cruising the flotsam like a pro, at ease,
But vulnerable, now. We wished him wary.

He was out word for 'nature', we didn't ask
To keep him, we didn't expect uniqueness,

There were no thanks in his luggage.
And perhaps he was no more wonderful than a seagull.
But I translated his visit as unique,
And it entered our language for the ferry back
And the holiday talk, and has never been forgotten.
Longer than usual I kept his souvenir,
An amazingly soft, un-icy, ice-white feather.
I'd stroke its length, brood about swansdown fillings,
And quill-pens trailing poems—all those uses—
And when it hurt I'd pause the reel, and stare
The feather to its flight-shape, white and far,
Like staring out a word until you see
The perfect strangeness. The spectacular silence.

BABY BABY BABY

Something's using them—stronger than their strong bodies,
their pierced, unforgettable bodies. When the boys complain
Oh, baby, baby, their searing laughter's the sign
it's begun to own them, Holy Ghost or goddess
they got for free—full power, no sacrifice.

Cameras enjoy them, evolution adores them,
their peach-bloom shoulders, eyes' immaculate punk
moons in each matched sunset of shadow and highlight.
Their blood roars round at such a lick that the junk
and the junk food and booze haven't scrawled one mark on them
yet.

Time has stood back for them, promised them a breather,
perhaps in a moment's weakness, perhaps because of a deal
with the power in them. Their minds are the lightest weather,
the landmass nobody worked or built on, primaeval.
You fear for them as they sashay across its fissures,

the terrible kneeling forms of the daddies and uncles
grabbing their ankles, howling, *Baby, we were joking*,
the thin white mother-claws wavering out of the funk-holes.
But they kick them to pulp, they're laughing, they chant love's
karaoke,
louder than anyone screams in a land still reckoned lucky.

They glow, and the power boots up to deliver more
life, lots more. Oh, baby, baby, baby, they wanted
to love you, although they dropped you in hard cots where
it frayed to wet rage. The power can't stop, they can't
stop it. The pills are forgotten, the condoms tear,

the power grins, *Yes!* And it coils in the girl-power thing.
It boils in the swaggering boys and the shag-each-other-to-bits
then-bash-each-other couples. The kids are swaying
their tiny peach-bloom shoulders, already certain it's
the only tune. *Oh, baby, baby*, it isn't—but it always is.

THE WEATHER OF SCARVES

We were playing at adultery when we swapped them
And smuggled them into our marriages.
They were the candid opposite of our bodies,
Our other clothes. They had no wrong-side-out.
Any bit of the fabric could have entered
That almond-sized hollow behind our ear-lobes,
Or buttercup-kissed a chin, or crept beneath
The hair to snuggle with a feathered nape,
They were perfect hands for sex, never tired or heavy,
Never ashamed. Their only wash was rain.

We left them in public places to betray us
But no one noticed, heard a single whisper.
Everything in the wedded world we gave them—
Our pheromones, our microbes, particles
Of street and work and skin, our spit and matter,
All the souls of our lives, each soul an odour—
Yet nothing. They were nothing,
A mood, a smoker's sigh. Their dream was breath:

They wished we free them from our weight and tangle,
Un-noose them, let them fly. And so with denser
Threads and knots of air they were re-woven

Until the time when we could cease pretending.
The smell of your life faded, there was only
An image, then, of chequered ash and sky,
Too long kept to be returnable.

THE GRANDMOTHER'S TALE

What I once loved were lies. They had such nice eyes!
In the ice of his smiles, I missed the truth by miles
But cornered my unicorn, marred and unmythically horned,
    And his word was my sword.

This is a route that's routinely unsuitable: bull-
At-a-gate while the *latte* is hot, and the candle-light flatters
The cad in your abracadabra, the hole in the whole simulacrum
    Of plenty in Lent,

You offer your coffers of treasure, and he goes 'Sure...'
So you buy him the Kohinoor. And it's wild for a while,
Until he ships out to his isle, and its single file
    From hypnotic to *not*.

But your heart says it's owed. This is so. From the day I was
        widowed,
Wed to his ghost, l soon hosted my own Casanova.
He leans from the empty chair, and his breath lifts my hair:
    'There, love, it's not over.'

Where are the old and their dead but enfolded in *ars amatoria*?
Faces and arms we embrace in the car parks of crematoria
Aren't mere remembrance: embraces evolve in us till
    The final nil-nil.

WATERCOLOUR

(late 20th Cent.)

The lake's a sampling of October:
Colour prints of rust and rose
And peach, no brighter, no more sober
Than the banked originals,
Call the lucky seaguils over:
Sky-branch, lake-branch, all are yours.

Clouds load in, dissolve, redouble,
Till they've stained the whole veneer,
Burst the frail mimetic bubble;
So our sun-struck heads-in-air
Find, these days, that mirrors trouble
Bright ideas of smiles and hair.

Does art age, as artists tend to?
Mimics' skills commence with eyes,
Eyes get misty. Minds extend few
Hooks to recent memories:
How can brushwork, then, pretend to
Visions and agilities?

We are rooted where time found us
Through a thousand strokes of luck,
Like the fruits cascading round us,
Most to perish where they struck:
Though the splitting seed feels boundless
Greenest days obey the clock.

Blind reporters, filming neither
Solid nor reflected things,
We might easier claim another
Life, complete with harps and wings,
Than convince the changing weather
We are where the new bird sings.

LULLABY AND WARNING

(to the Field at Buarth Gwarchau)

Pause, field, each time the sky
Fails to dawn through its dulled
Barley haze, mysteriously like yours.
Earth has begun to separate from light
And though your grass-mind whispers, 'It's all right,
The usual separation, not divorce,'
Few businesses, you know, in your vast city,
Won't rationalise or fold.

The playground's destitute.
Your prettiest strippers, stripped from crown to root,
Can find no shoppers:
The tiny dealers, with their deely-boppers,
Tail-coats and shades,
Who cruised the gorgeous spectra, scored, sold on
The surplus bullion,
Freeze, now, in scentless beds.

But crust this scythe,
Its steel exactness, simplifying, clearing,
As necessary as breath.
And if it fails, because bad tenants spoiled
The sky, blunted the blade,
And goad you with their winter-free design,
Pause, field. A stalled September isn't spring.
No root of you should stretch. No stem should shine.

WELSH STREAM

We heard no watery rustle, saw no movement
at first. And then we spotted it, the tic,
the one-nerve flicker, every thirty seconds,
and knew, with an absurd sense of reprieve,
that the dead muscle, brown as parcel-seal,
where clay sagged at the weight of fern and horsetail,
was in fact living water, weak but striving
with tiny shudders for a different place.
To bond with the Basques. And though the Eistedfodd boys (sorry)
Won't ever invite them, there will be plenty more platforms
To win in their own wonder category: English Welsh Writer in English.

DO THE SERIAL MONOGAMISTS NEED A NEW VOCABULARY?

Love's the word we use when the urge takes us
Above the clouds in piercing claws, and fakes us
A crown of stars. 'I love him/her to bits'
We say, showing how well the L-word sits
With GBH. Love has no qualms. It bakes us

A pie of children's hearts. Oh, but it wakes us
So gently, whispering, stroking. It re-makes us
Into the small fair-headed one, who fits
All kisses. When we write our greatest hits,
Love's the word we use.

Love justifies our sperm, our spawn, our acres,
And when, one day, betrayal or boredom rakes us,
And old names are spat out like bitter pits,
We mouth the sweet new flavour, swearing it's . . .
(Love's the word we use).

FINISHING A POEM CAN BE LIKE THIS, TOO

Though the Nuns said they had no souls
We kids gave fancy burials
To birds and voles,

Laid them in lint and prayed that broad-
Church angels might put in a word
For them with God.

Whereof we cannot speak, keep talking, softly:
One howl awaits the mouths that make the holes
Made by their masters' mouths, at first with laughter,
Later, slack consent. Try 'no' again, and savour
The difference from their 'yes'. Words last a generation,

And only while our children still confirm the flavour.

DE-CREATION 2004

Think of a face
That bites its lip and twists its brow to bind
Closed eyes in place.

Over the brow, a hand
Searches the seam where bone and tissue, spurred
Viciously, fused into mind,

A hand like an absently-fathered
Cradle-word, half curse.
Repeated again and again, or the sullen tread

Of troops, unwinding the wars.
So the waters between them turned.
Again into blood or shivering truce: not yours.

You prayed for rain, you were burned
To ash. In the only dream
Again and again you are orphaned.

You play being her, being him,
Being loved by a god. But the child is always dead
Between them—between the leather-stain of her palm
And his tethered head.

Today less piety informs
My shovelling into roots' and worms'
Tight catacombs

Until I've made a sort of nest,
Deep, damp and cold, for the fluffed breast
And school-cap crest,

Grieved that such colours, cornsilk bright,
The passerine finesse of flight,
Have lost their light

Yet not unconscious of the thrill
Of something near impalpable
Brought down, stopped still.

from **Blind Spots** (2008)

BETWEEN TWO WARS

Roots are not easily killed, in spite of tank-tracks
and trenches; birds, years later, perch above battle-fields.
What if in city courtyards the grey grass almost mocks
its own entitlement? All poetry yields
to grass, all grass to photosynthesis.
And the poet's senses warm themselves like mud-larks
in trivia: the reeds' wisp-bearded profile,
Isis, tipping her slops, trampling her polythene laundry,
swags of stink, iridescent effluvia.
New light does not dawn lightly in this country
of midday dusks and hanging air. What else
but fall in love with a man or a lemon-tree?
I wander home with my heightened pulse, my notions,
and when I've found their silvery web-page, those
guests of a guess, your words, will keep their coats on –
as he, of course, will, as the unhappy tree will.
Trees are too slow. I want the bird-bright coif
or spear of colour, now—kingfisher, saffron, snow,
poinsettia-crimson. Light-creators, glow,
pull me towards your heavy mouths until
the day grows younger, taller—and old age detests itself.

DOUBLED SOLSTICE

Love, which restores in us the needs of children
So that new children may be created,
One day mistakes a winter's afternoon

For spring. A butterfly quakes into the frozen
Air, bees dander from lost head to head;
And love, that swears it has no need of children,

Emboldens us to wrap ourselves in skin
Not wholly like our own, to be enfolded
And naked on a winter's afternoon.

We can explain this chemistry-in-a-cauldron,
Dismiss the levitation of the dead,
But love, mocked by the piercing needs of children,

Puts back the clocks we trust, declares it dawn
At midnight, shakes our sense of the absurd:
Tender mistakes of summer snow at noon,

Seeds from frost-flowers, mistletoe on the moon.
Oh bower-bird, dancing in a factory yard,
Oh love, you bring to age the tears of children,
Your longest day to winter's afternoon.

THE THRESHOLD

You took my hand and pressed it to the heartbeat
under your shirt   I was afraid for both creatures,
and again I remembered the young house-martin
throwing its horrified exclamation-mark
at the trompe l'oeil of a rather dirty window.
I couldn't   had to   catch
            couldn't   had to   keep hold of
the breakable wings, so wild to sweep that thunder
of heartbeat into sky. My palms closed over
the sleek crisp dried-ink feathers, and fell open.
Astounded, at the threshold, we stood still.

LITTLE EPIC

('L'anguilla, torcia, frusta,
freccia d'Amore in terra,' *L'anguilla* *)

Everything was yet to be imagined—
even the river with her sandy blushes,
slithering up the chrome-work barrier,
and the bridge, that heron slenderness, its soaring
cruelly earthed by strings of disguised rain;
motor-ways, beach-walks—vanishing perspectives
of latitude—all were un-measured since
geography had never heard of you;
and nothing in the six-fold darkness stirred.
A god can have his project almost finished
before he lights upon that little spiral
of mud which seethes it into sense, but I,
the lesser maker, needed last things first:
before the supernovae, clouds, volcanoes
and icebergs—Adam! Stealthily engraved
(work of a star, perhaps, I dared not ask)
a human symbol lit the stone. The river
edged around it, birds hovered above it:
museums were bright with fish, shopping-malls claimed the sea.
Everything was more itself since printed
with some line trace of him; even the air
feathered uncertainly into a footprint.
Then, like the washed-up oil-drum, swamped and emptied
with every tide, I tried to turn aslant
and rest—but from no angle could refuse it—
sea-fire and lash and squalor of love's earthing.
which crashed the floodgates and, when it receded,
left nothing like a world. Left bridgeless dust.

(*'Eel, torch, whiplash, arrow /of love on earth'-*The Eel*, Jonathan Galassi, trans.)

THE READING-LAMP SONOGRAM

I cannot hear you, no—
the light-streaked ash-white margins, the black letters
are not your keyboard:
your thoughts are not soft plectra on the graded strings.

But the silence sings to itself, as happiness does.
I creak my chair, skim pages, talk a little.
It is a blessing and an exorcism
to let slip, in my migrant worker's tongue,
the possibly excessive confirmation:

Ma è possibile,
lo sai, amare un' ombra . . .'

Eavesdropping on love, my listening eyes
strain like October leaves before
the decimation,
brimming with rainbows, making waves—
so summer-fed they can't quite own their dying.

You know, it's not your voice alone they print
in me, nor simply mine:
something is outlined, though, as we gather these

co-ordinates of frequency,
time
and intensity –

some shadowy peculiar composite
of swimmer wrapped in sleeper,
answer bound into question, work so complex,

it asks a dual creator
but only one to bear it,
to rock it in her secret resonant fluids . . .

oh silent child, oh silent child

(Stanza 2, incomplete quotation from "Xenia 1", Poem 13: "But it is possible/ you know, to love a ghost, ghosts that we ourselves are" .Tr. Jonathan Galassi.)

SHADES

'. . . Or puoi la quantitate/ comprender de l'amor ch'a te mi scalda,/
quand'io dismento nostra vanitate,/trattando l'ombre come cosa salda.'*
(Dante, Canto xxi, *Purgatorio*, spoken by Statius to Virgil.)

There is a hell with not a single soul,
Local or tourist, nosing through its murk:
This is the myth that 'hell is other people'—

The writer's myth. The loneliness we make
Encircles us; we sink in the defeat,
Displacing muddy towers we call our work.

But you, disgruntled shade, I hoped to meet
In some bleak bay, threading the needle's eye
Of scholarship with posthumous lantern-light.

I would have known you if you'd drifted by,
And, seeing as I'm not entirely dead,
I would have drawn my sigh across your sigh,

And breathed some heavier warmth. Montale said
In his long conversation with the past,
'It's possible, you know, to love a shade.'

I'm not saying you would have paused, or noticed –
Even when, in some trickery of desire,
Your smile was by a stranger's smile replaced.

What use are smiles? Hell is a private fire –
Unlike the world, peopled and merely warm –
And coveting faint shades, a poor career
Although we burn so hard we give them form.

*(". . . Now you understand/ how much my love for you burns deep in me,
I when I forget about our emptiness//and deal with shadows as with solid things."
- Trans. Mark Musa.)

POETRY

('La poesia e la fogna, due problemi mai disgiuoti . . .'
-'Poetry and the sewer, two inseparable problems'
'Dopo una fuga'—*Satura* 11,Trans. William Arrowsmith)

This river, no more distinguished than the large intestine,
no less mysterious
with its bacterial pastoral
only the sacrilegious attempt
to catalogue, its sump-pool
glittering with black reeds and a rusted swan—

we did not give our lives to it:
we had no life without it.

SECOND HEART

I grope back;
tearing through the web of sixty years—

my webbed, sixty-years-old, beginning-to-tear hand

past the spinning figures
of the nearly-young, who jump away
to the trembling edges, afraid,
a little afraid they might see themselves inside it

but my hand's not clawed, its feelers are pianissimo,

scaling the shyness of a broken chord,
light as shed skin-cells,
till it meets, swimming along the Milky Way,
a fist that splashes, spangles,

shows its span of miniature iris-bloom nails,
polished by barely sixty dawns—and not a single crime
under the faintly-inscribed, articulate,
sea-clean, shrimp-shell fingers.

New Hand doesn't fear Old Hand,
but seizes it and smothers it—as much of it as she can—
in a bone-gummed, lippy slobber
until it almost melts,
melts into mouth, into baby.

Painter of eyes, grasper of nettles, money-masseuse,
reviser of stories—my hand

folded away in the dream-time,
practising dunes and tunnels, branchy sleep-forms—
a webby, double-chambered, pulsing sci-fi organ

that thrills awake to what pulls
against it, the fat sea
at the slip-down shore, the sea-anemone

that's almost solid tongue—my hand, licked clean,
new-born, with a small second heart.

ON BEING (SOMETIMES) VERTICAL AND VERBAL

What on earth is it that explains our gait?
Even in coupled poise we walk half-cock
And crabbed with verbs: *regret, anticipate.*

That leaves explain how cups originate,
And sunlight on a swirl of crags, the clock,
Is clear, but what on earth explains our gait?

Our soles plod on. Meanwhile, our palms vibrate
With cunning voices, digits, tones, caps lock,
The lexis of young verbs: *text, network, date.*

Did brains refine our paws, or hands add freight
To brains? Do our pained feet insist we talk,
Or is it language that explains our gait?

And still we genuflect, or fall prostrate
To gods we've carved ourselves from logs or rock:
Why do we serve, who also say 'check mate?'

Hands are our learning outcomes, but too late.
Old hands make gardens grow. Little hands walk
At dawn. The want of earth explains our gait,
Our lonesome hands that plead *explain, translate.*

A CALEPIN FOR DR. BREWER

Aretinian Syllables, sing
To our Bevy of sky-sipping, 'timid,
Gregarious' **Candidates** ('Lat. *Candidatus*, clothed
In white'). **Not for donkey's years** have we dreamed
Of **Evans's Supper Rooms**, where the air blushed blue,
Refurbished , and our **Familiar** of Assisi,
Home from the **Glubbdubdrib Hock-shop**,
Poorer than **Irus**, back in his *Portiuncula*.
Jubilee Juggins, skint, squeezes a glad concertina
Again on the swaying **Knifeboard**,
And they creep, the little draped **Larvae**, as ever,
Who have no **Monument** ,
And long for **New Learning**, the sun on the olive-skin,
Not the stone in the **Olla Podrida**.
Gather them in a **Pavan**
Or a poem that bets its soul on **Quiddity**
Or a picture of health, where **Raphael**, 'sociable spirit,'
Munches his fish on someone's **Sarcophagus**,
Conjuring up a **Theophany** ('see
TIFFANY') and **Uncumber, St.** decides
To shave off her beard for a little **Vis à Vis**
'Properly applied.' Feed us **Wind-eggs**. Wire us
Your almost-guessable mysteries, **Abe to Zebi**.
Let all be **Yclept** until **Yggdrasil**, 'tree of knowledge
And time and space,' with its 'fountain of wonderful virtue,'
Roots and branches once more,
In earth as it is in **Zeugma**,
Dear Dr. Brewer!

(All definitions are from Brewer's *Dictionary of Phrase and Fable*, Centenary Edition, 1970, revised by Ivor H. Evans, Cassell, London.)

CLOTHES LEFT ON A WASHING-LINE

in the Gaza Strip, 2005

What could we do, when the Jews came for the Jews
to tell them there is no God,
there are no miracles?

We hung, collars down, in the usual manner,
motionless in the sun, our dyes blazing
like the peonies and jacaranda
planted all round us by our clever weavers
as they went on giving God the credit for everything—
the desert, the city, even the rotary clothes-line.
We hung together, helpless when their fury
shook us like an unfamiliar wind.
They howled they were coming back, they were going to feed us
again their hard strong lives, their strenuous occupation.
We, who had shielded their bodies,
couldn't cover up this stupidity.
Forgive us, but we're clothes, not flags: we're realists.

And when the Palestinians come
to tear us from our pegs and make a bonfire,
happy that we're so shallow and boneless and wicked,
we'll tell them exactly what the Jews told the Jews:
there is no God, there are no miracles.

LONDON STONE

They were young, war was new, it was nylons
and lippie, and drinks on the house
in the Strand, in a place called the Coal Hole.

They drank Gin and It till they spun,
and the warrior, scrubbing her kiss
with his wet, red knuckle, ran

over the cobbles to Charing Cross Station
where soldiers were roaring like coal
down the dirty old throat of the coal-hole,

and the warrior's woman decanted
her drink in the palm-pot and swayed
through the dawn with the glow of a bride

already, to win the new war,
a stone's throw away, where the poor were,
where it licked up the high streets, still hungry.

London, you can't have forgotten.
Haven't your books got no pages –
or did you just rip out the pages

about what the bombs do in bomb-holes,
the cute little fox in his fox-hole,
and the hero who hoots from the hell-hole.

The bartender's sixty years late, wasn't born.
though he knows the word, Blitz—it's a cocktail,
and everyone's sixty years late and not born

and we go with the flow in the Coal Hole,
where nothing's been changed since the Tudors
and history's only a tart with no heart

in her brass and mahogany boudoir,
making the poor blighters poorer.
So where's the way out? And the hole,

the hole we go down in, and when's
the train coming, the tram we go home in
after we've started the stoning?

Stone is the way, let me show you.
Stone, where no stone was before.
Stone from the optics and fountains,

stone for the walkers and sleepers,
stone for the strikers, the same for the suckers,
stone for their bodies to melt in,

stone for the myth to be built on.

Stone for the soot-flakes to fall on

when all the stone has fallen.

A BERTH FOR THE SHIPPING CLERK

As I walked out on London Bridge
One misty morning early (1)
I was one of the millions milling the shilling
To keep the windlass turning.

But where did he go, with his shy ducking movement,
His glance ironic, hopeful? Into which mooring?
Billeter Street, a secret hammock strung
From bank to river-bank, twists with dreams of him.
Hopeful, ironic, I conjure him across
A sea of messenger bikes. He disappears and the traffic
Sings *toomer loomer loomer, toomer loomer loomer*. *(2)*

Up the steps of Dock House, straightening his smile, his tie,
He sprints like a boy. Dock House? In Port Sudan
Or Surrey, there's a drifty mind, turning
Its private globe where the empire steams and streams
Like cooks' pink custard (magic!) over school grub.
There floats Dock House off-shore, distinctly misty.
It was Victorian Venice. It was pure music-hall.

Can a building be a ghost? Turn up the gaslight
Under the pavement, let it whoosh and wobble
A passing sea-light over Thames-brown screens
Where traders click and flick the digital words—
Ports, documents, windows—shades of their analogue selves.
Puff Daddy in the basement gym goes *umber*
Umber umber umber umber.
The treadmills mill young muscle-fibre finer
But the scribbler at his desk is practising
('Dear Sirs, we write regretfully to inform you')
His *toomer loomer loomer* and his *toodle oomer oomer*.

Dock House was blitzed, the freight company moved
Into passenger shipping and sank—a few white streets along.
But all his life I believed in that address.
At thirty, I could have run to the top of the tumbled stairs
And found him there, doodling towards retirement:
Pitter patter patter, pitter patter patter, here comes the rain
Let it pitter patter, let it pitter patter, don't mind the rain

Typical parent—he died before we met.
In Fenchurch Street I caught him at the station
(Its cable-cars the quietest trains in London)
And pounced. I dared his ghost. 'Remember the foolscap pads
You nicked for me—and the German typewriter?
I never retired.' And we ducked into Books, Etc.
To broker a tiny connection in this city of et ceteras.

A few Penguins and Fabers rode the shallows.
Birthday Letters, of course. 'A fantastic love-story'
Said a careful biro on the staff-pick postcard
Brown as old steamship galleys, the lunchtime pubs
Were heaving to as we surfaced, the un-published
And the out-of-print.
Oh poetry-scribbling clerks, oh would-be song-and-dance-men
Who's to say you were less than laureates
And in your secret loves—they, too, fantastic—
And states of utmost doubt, made nothing happen?
How quickly, without love, though we work, we fade.
Loved too, we work and fade. Time for a quick one?

So we turned down Lime Street Passage into the watery shadows
Glass distils from light, two soft-shoe-shufflers—*he*
Will mend them all

With what he calls
A thingummyjig
In soft Bud Flanagan voices. Clannish shippers,
Taking the micky, shouted, 'What'll you have, Bill?
Malay, Khartown, the White Nile or the Blue?'

Something like that, he said, and looked as distant
As Saturday to Monday.
It was then
My hand merged into his, since both had nearly vanished.
There was a bus and we took it
Over London Bridge, to the slummy south,
To the gasoliers and the sticky plush and the ashtrays,
To the Lewisham Hippodrome: Saturday everlasting
For the clerks who never rose from under the pavements,
From the treadmills' gasp—except as puffs of song.

Toomer loomer loomer, toomer loomer loomer
Toomer ly aye
I was one millionth, milling the shilling
Day after day,
Humming those ditties, I stuck like the Thames to its toiling,
And with ' umberellas any umberellas' wore time away.

(l) "Geordie", tradirional English folksong.
(2) These and other italicised lines are from "The Umbrella Man" by Flanagan and Allen.

BABY TALK

(for Yura)

1.
It was forbidden. My mother said
If you can say 'gee-gee' you can say 'horse'.
If you can say 'woof-woof', of course,
You can say 'dog'. You go to 'bed'
Not 'bye-byes'. 'Wee-wee' was whackable, 'poo-poo' a no-no –
And what a disgrace, to ask for a drink of 'wo-wo'.
But I trotted a *Mobo Bronco*, and raced my *Chuff-Chuff* trains.
Not baby-talk. Brand-names.

2.
To you, it's permitted. *Kartoshichki*: spuds under pink-flowered soil
Or naked in the saucepan, under a cloud.
Gribki sa smetanoe: mushrooms with cream. The letters of Lili Brik
And Vladimir Mayakovsky, where they bill
And coo and sign off, depending on the mood,
As 'Zverik' (little beast), 'Lilik', 'Volosik.'

ALMOST TRUE: A GUIDED WALK THROUGH LARKIN'S COTTINGHAM

They gathered in the rainy village, muses
And friends who had outlived you, 'getting on,'
As they'd have said, no longer latest faces.
   Kind arm and walking-stick
Led them, as they led us, to church or green,
And time's tough skin proved curiously elastic.

Recovering the shapes you'd first assigned them,
They blushed in your short-sighted, dreamy gaze.
One read out 'Afternoons', one, 'Wedding Wind'.
   An unambiguous friend
Stepped forward and displayed a shapeless tee-shirt
On whose blue front she'd printed all of 'Days'.

They talked us through their stories, gentle, clear,
Amused if they recalled a quirk or fault,
And it was only gradually that I
   Who'd wished, but never felt
The slightest breath or tremor of you, though
I'd walked your vanished footprints for a year,

Became aware of something, an attention,
Aloof, but faintly warming. The shy fury
Of rain drummed our umbrellas. We were shown
   The playground, small and glum—
Location, 'so Maeve said', of 'Afternoons.'
And birds seemed to make merry with the query,

What will survive? The work of course, we cried,
The work. But every instinct understood
How tenderly, to those with whom you'd shared
   Mere life, you would have turned,
And vanished through the dusk of memory, leaving
The experts to debate the barely heard.

COATS

Once I mistook a mourner for a stone.
Her short dark coat contained a self so still
I thought her face a flower, a tied-on balloon.

People are mostly taller than their small
Secular polished slabs, but often they
Bend down to rearrange the gnomes or pull

A weed, and I expect they nearly pray.
And so it happens: people seem the size
Of gravestones, and it's hard to turn away

Because I trust and do not trust my eyes
When stones begin to stumble and turn right
Towards the crematorium. I surmise,

In fact, all stones are coat-clad bodies, white
Or black, convivial or fighting shy,
Superior with button-holes or bright

Tinsel trim. Their limbs, rocked in, keep dry.
They hood their little skulls against the cold,
And hunch beside the beds in which they'll lie,

At dusk, leaving the coats they never fold,
Draped on the head-boards, ready to put on
Next time they're summoned to identify
A mourner by her new cold coat of stone.

WOMEN, VEILED

Because the mouth has been known to tell lies
Because beauty isn't better than compassion
Because we live with two terrors: being looked at, not being looked at
Because we shine without photosynthesis.

Because our eyes are lost birds, beating from dark to dark
Because our foreheads were scorched by the explosion
Because you need room for your house, when you must leave it
And because we mourn for the children, butchered in Crazy Park.

And because you should give death time, though your body blooms
with plenty
Because you are mostly liquid. Because you need somewhere to laugh
Because you're the sleeve of Allah. Because of the man you have chosen
Because he is simple. Because you have chosen yourself

AFTER A DELUGE

'The book itself is only a tissue of signs... The structure can be run (like the thread of a stocking) at every point and at every level, but there is nothing underneath.' (Roland Barthes)

The city's drainage ran
by tidal authority
but some tides took scant notice
of essential services.
No less an authority
than the weather, ran
the revised transport services.
Microbes were pleased to notice
these shifts of authority
as dinner services
and sofas ran;
and lavatories gave notice.
The Evacuation Services,
high-viz with authority,
proclaimed their ferries ran
on time, put up a notice.
We admired the new services.
At first, we didn't notice
any lapse of authority.
The flood-waters ran
silver-soft, an *in memoriam* notice
fluttered with flowers. Desire services
belief. If our ark ran
aground without our authority
we were the last to notice.
Our conversations ran

on Machine Translation, Methodist services
and the British Airports Authority
  Rainy the sweet inks ran
like nylons, whispered 'Notice
our ark of signs, our deathless authority.'
We dispensed with their services.

THE GREENFINCH

Up where the birch-tree's fine bronze veins fan out
and up, and the tiny frilled
hands go crazy – spinning, spinning
swee a swee
till they drop from their thready wrists
and up

swee a swee

through the rigging and rigmarole – and all the way
up through the emerald-mines in the still
high-lighted canopy *swee a swee tswee tswee*
it's as if
as if
a string of greenish spit a splash of yellowish shit
was flicked at the sky and
split

into two wings, cartoonish, quickly
bird bird that quirkily
perched for a sec (never wert? – saw it whole!)
blacky-whitey tail seed-cracker beak
then sideways
into the tasselled Byzantium of
cypress
shot off, and among
the spirally networked stairways tumbled slightly *screea cree scree cree*
cree
fell to soft nattering, settled
like a bark-flake, darkly

creea cree

cree cree

fining down

from wing-flash and feather-fuss, down

to an eye   to an eye

to a *peck*

peck

peck

all's soundless now but the soft bees at their harvest

WALKING ON HAIL-STONES

(For Isabella)

('Al poco. giorno, e el gran cerchio d'ombra'—Dante, *The Rime Petrost)*

To shorter days and globe-dividing shadow
She's travelled from no farther than last April,
And while we dine, oblivious to the human
Extreme called Christmas, she, wise Isabella,
Dozes, and charms the dads and childless women,
As hailstones melt against the tinselled window.

Leave her content behind her buggy window!
We're in the car-park. Harsh beams splice the shadow.
I've said I'll walk her home. Yes, I'm a woman
Who walks, and on this clear but far-from-April
Night, not out of love for Isabella
Alone, I want the chill of things pre-human—

Black hush, brash glitz of stars. Perhaps that's human.
The car brrmms past, Kelsey winds down the window:
'Hey, Mum. Take care!' I'll try to, Isabella.
Turning the buggy, turning into shadow
Untouched by stars, I murmur, 'whan that April
With his shoures soot . . .' and men and women

Pour out of Southwerk, motley nattering women
And blathering blokes – not epic, merely human –
But move they'd swear, by light bigger than April.
Let's say we're pilgrims in a different window
Of faith. The gods have gone. They leave scant shadow
But grief, and children, dear as Isabella,

Sprawled by their broken cisterns. Isabella,
Not every track dips homeward. Children, women,
Cross borders in their millions and in shadow
(That's the quirked certainty of upright human).
Our worst is this – to shake like unlatched windows
In gales that want a bust-up before April.

PERHAPS

Floodwater drying on a field
assumes the rough-torn-paper shapes
of countries, islands, continents –
Africas and Gaza Strips
alike, shrunk and abandoned, filled
with drifts of cloud, some eggshell sky,
as if the final ice had flowed,
and life and all its stains and rents
were gassy shimmer, mere *perhaps*.

from **De Chirico's Threads**

(2010)

1. THE BIRTH OF VENUS

'I can tell from here what the inhabitants of Venus are like; they resemble the Moors of Granada; a small black people, burned by the sun, full of wit and fire, always in love, writing verse, fond of music, arranging festivals, dances, and tournaments every day.'– Bernard de Foncenelle, 1686.

Bernard de Fontenelle, you took a shine
To Venus, but we've learned a thing or two
Since then. She's mostly cracked volcanic plain,
Her clouds are sulphur (pray they never rain)
And though the Hubble's filter bathes her blue,
Her oceans warmed and went. Oh, world of dew!

She warns us: cool it. Yet, as your eyes wished her
Life, so we construct her centre-fold
Of continents into the foamy world
Of Terra Aphrodite, Terra Ishtar,
As if such radiance figured potency—
Love-comet Zeus not taking no, the shroud
Slick with glycine. Sea or no sea,
Boars burn for Venus still. And gods are formed from cloud.

2. ALBA

It was this morning's REM sleep, and the dream
Began in Kwiksell, or was it Costsaver?
I was near the check-out when, from another room,
He beckoned, held out a gift: *lactuca sativa*!
It was my boss. I was pale and dumb as a foetus,
And filmed with milky saliva
As I stretched my hand to the globe of his home-grown lettuce.

Though I stalked him all day in the annex of Human Resources,
He had far too much on his place
To observe the green gleam of my glances.
Oh, let me dream more and lie late,
Till our fingers melt through the lattice
Of leaves, and he beckons me onto his office-lounger,
And offers my lips his salad-bowl, *prêt-à-manger*.

3. THE SOLDIER'S GIRL-FRIEND

Call-up. And it's as if I'd never met him
And wouldn't want to. Others wave goodbye.
I'm hanky-less and dry.
My simple transitives? Dump him or regret him.

I dreamed I found his tent on the front-line.
His face was stitched. His penis would have failed
The *pleased-to-see-me* test. He hasn't emailed . . .
His war has no intelligence of mine.

I google LOVE POEMS, savour crushed desire:
Our courtship, whose whole concept's mediaeval.
Shivers between Petrarch's ice and fire.

Girls with *intelligence of love*, compare
His tropes with what the literal-minded bomber:
Does with the pearls and rubies a young man's summer.

7. THEATRES

Wed to his roadside slut, my husband came
Home in that awful suit-case. Massive-shouldered,
He walked on smaller shoulders
Until he slipped and darkened. I became

A tower of speaking flame, a lilied angel,
Who blushed and looked translucent without help
From Makeup. Tears made little pearls. That helped.
I saw myself divine from every angle.

And all the media trusting me to play
My part, the starry part a young girls owed,
If she's a woman widowed,

her leading man all crammed with lead. Some play!
I court the camera's I.E.D. like he
crawled to that bitch. Theatre's in our blood.

8. THE WHITE STAG

It was the bitter season, early spring.
At sunrise, on some laurel-shaded grass,
Islanded where the two rivers pass,
A white stag, golden-horned, stood quivering.

Charmed by his glances, I dropped everything
And hurried after him. Bankers amass
Their wealth by being similarly ruthless,
The tough work eased by money's pleasant ring.

Closing in, as his handsome throat turned,
I saw inscribed in diamonds and warm topaz:
'Don't touch! This deer belongs to Caesar's herd.'

It was already noon, the sun had burned
Westward; still I couldn't rest my eyes
Till water drowned them, and he disappeared.

'The White Stag' is a re-working of Petrarch's 'Una Candida Cerva' (*Rime* 190).

DIPHTHONGS

In labour you grow old
you listen to the pain   you give it room
  to stretch a little wider and a little
            wider till it tears a noise from you
that's not the child unless
              the child is pain

You're interested at first   surprised to learn
  nature has set no limits
  your body though you love it   sets no limits
    but tricks you with a little
    easy pain that's the beginning of
          a wave that won't stop gathering when you say

   enough
                        fold back give
   over

pain doesn't hesitate because a forehead
      shines or breath is
      harsh. Pain has its say   it burns
  enormous holes through prayers. *Pain will learn you.*

There are such diphthongs in the word   pain
          you're opening like the future
                  and all it says is death
and death's like this
          perhaps
              or dying is
But this

time it's not death. Remember
the other meaning   breathe it   rhyme it further
and harder   wider   harder   till wide
nature
is satisfied   closes her golden eye
relents. Your turn.
You turn

THE WOBBLE

There are some minds happiest among archives.
We track their progress through the world of crude,
Their quick adjustments, their refined evasions,
When offered to the battlefields where treason
Itself may not be strategy enough.
We watch with shy concern, the way you watch
A small child standing on a swivel-chair.
You grip the seat, she flies above the keyboard,
Chagall-like. From her hands, the star-tailed data
Evolve and swim. To such an art of balance—
To such an art—the wobble's integral.
There are some minds so happy among archives
They dance there sometimes, witty as their toes.

THE OLD CRYSTAL PALACE 'HIGH LEVEL' STATION

Migrants have drifted in steadily for years.
They crowd the crumpling platform, recycle the sleepers.
The bright tin signs, in a humble, grassier language,
stutter *Alight Here for the Crystal Palace.*

A tossed-away fag, my father surmised, ignoring
the sabotage theories, had brought it down like a bomb.
There were craters and blackened echoes in my time,
and meadow blues: then the floodlit stadium, roaring.

I haunted its afterlife, the toppled heads
of plaster-cast Rome, or the disappointing maze.
In the High Level Station, still, the ballroom staircase,
crinoline wide, meets a high five of colonnades,

but only the pigeons commute. They bustle and moan,
and the station waits like a soldier in a skirt,
staring at no horizon, holding the fort
on the tip of his spear—a sweetmeat for an old woman

forever his pudding-faced queen. The 'hollow square'
dissolves, the bricks shimmer off to the latest theatre:
More men, we must have more! So the legionnaires—
'the long and the short and the tall'—flow through the timer

like sand, like flame through stockades, like ripples unfurled
on the leaden lake where a child chucked stones at nothing,
and the planters puff on their Players and Senior Service.
Preserve it—our beautiful record of ruling the world—

and polish the redbrick and terracotta tiles
till they show us how empty the turreted booking-hall
where the shop boys scrapped and cheered, ghost armies just out of school,
arriving on cheap day-returns with their straw-hatted girls

at the foot of the twentieth century, running too fast
up the ever-steepening steps, *get a load of them crystals*
and nick one, Bill, if we're lucky. They spin through the echoing portals.
Fresh grass breaks stones. Ozymandias forms out of dust.

THE CONCENTRATION-CAMP POPLARS REMEMBER THEIR FIRST GARDENERS

Because they had to be slaves before they died,
their hands were used, their feet were used, their spines
were bent and used, their breath was pumped, pumped,
pumped till the valves failed, their sweat was forced
or tricked from them, like their last spoon or shoe.

The grass is too young to be a suspect:
the signposts and the freshly surfaced walkways
that whisper, *you weren't born*, weren't born. But we—
choice seedlings for a smoke screen (uprooted
like them, half-dead, like them)—we let them spill us
among the rocks they'd cursed and brashed that day.
Some were no longer standing. Some could kneel.

Their fingers chilled us, but they pushed us down,
down, our roots found soil. We sucked the ram
which, when they'd left, fell thickly with their falling.
Then, one by one we raised our arms, confessing
the stolen jewels, their lives. We could not shed them.

They grow in us. We pray our aching branches
may ferry them to the leaf tips of your blindness.

HURBINEK'S CHILDREN

i.m. the Rememberer, Primo Levi

Hurbinek, no one's left to help you repeat
Your word, the first you tried.
You were born in hell. None of us could translate,
Though we speak so much, such a word.

On your arm's small L, a tattoo,
Full-sized. In your dark eyes' O, the hoard
Of life, all wasted. Who
Had scratched the word on the void

Of your brain? One who was kind?
Was anyone kind? What a language you'd have had,
If you'd kept on trying to find

Your tongue, till the hell sprang through
Your vocal chords, Hurbinek, and you knew
There was a language everyone understood.

Note: in *The Truce: A Survivor's Journey from Auschwitz*, Primo Levi wrote of the three-year-old Auschwitz survivor known as Hurbinek: 'He died in the first days of March 1945, free but not redeemed. Nothing remains of him: he bears witness through these words of mine.'

SHAPED MATTER

*Poem beginning with an idea from Rilke's 'An Holderlin'**

We're not allowed to stay, no, not among
The most familiar things . . . These things may change
Their terms with us, however, and our lightest
Shadow, farthest cast, disturb or mist them.
Returning home, we grope for sameness, checking
Hen-heartedly that nothing's shattered, stolen
Or stone: only the kid are disappointed!
But gradually we notice a faint bruising
Or minor lesion – bloody work of absence
As it keeps playing catch with bloodless things.
We're not supposed to linger – but we linger,
Settling our toys and penny fairings, till they're
Leaning towards our myth. They're beautiful
Once more, because they bore us. Lust for boredom
Is why we linger with the beautiful.

Consider, from all those, the one person
Whose looks, so deeply known, you'll never know.
That poignant face went by. What's left but shorthand?
A few strokes we call metonymy—
The bored perfection of our editorship.
So we start work on love, curtailing, pinching
Its edges to the semblance of a thing,
A charm against all absence—faultless sameness.
We stay, we linger, knowing love is nothing
But matter wanting to be changed and slowly
Lost. We think by touching less we keep it.

* 'Abiding, not even in what we know best / is given us . . .'
-(Trans. David Constantine)

RIDDLE

you were the glowing inks a punch-drunk God
smeared for his pledge: the bow
he slung away, laughing.
                                        Gold-medal sprinter,
you gave the slip to earth-sky frontiers: gently
you widened Dido's wound, knowing the skills
of the hospice as a sideline,
and lowered yourself to rumour – grubby gold:
we still forgave your teasing

until   our deeper looking   teased you back and tore

fatally
your see-through silk   we traced your

scar of   light's   slow   travel

(slow!)   through thickset air

on a rain-drop's shell, you turned

in a moment's fading, faded

we handled you
phenomenon   knifed you open

somewhereover   never-land   we dropped
you

un-done your eight-fold

cloth all holed

your ribboned skin
all the more wonderful, we said.

And seemingly you magnify us still:
you stretch the water in our eyes; glance over
our domes and spires, un-mocking. You could still lean down,
Iris, and have mercy on the world.

THE MUDSTONE RAINBOW

Lake Ogwen, February

I waded out into the lake,
Panning for scraps of pearly grit;
And here's my catch—a brown mosaic
Of mudstones that deny all light
If water fails to mediate.
Their dripping, rusty slivers leave
Henna'd fingers, a soaked sleeve,
But something bare and true to like.

The flat-topped mountain's scimitar
Presses the sky and turns it pale.
That curve, those melting bands, compose
A modest rainbow of the soil,
No flame of green in it, scant rose:
From frosty grass to distant shale
It shrugs at what the water does
With wobbled shadow, hints of star.

Temples, I think, will never shine
Out of this earth, though houses might.
It seems a scrap-yard of lost time
When splats of refuse cleverly leapt
As handles into hands, as blades
Into the blood. Those Stone-Age shades
Take aim. The unknown alphabets
Spell fear, the known lie readerless.

Back to the stones. I brought them home,
Designer Paleozoic slate!
Restful, dusty, now room-warm,
Most of their fire and ice played out,
They promise nothing rainbow-bright
But silently amalgamate
The mystery of the last sea-bed
To mountains formed inside the head.

2084

Paired wheels and PV panels, ponds and hives
and garden-fields (citron and silvery-green
samplers, all hand-stitched) declare our ground.
We're scripture-safe: for each estate, one screen
only, daily rationing of down-loads.
That ice-bar, frilling in the distant sound,
that flood, in motion inches from the cross-roads
where we abolished runways and re-wound
the windmills, will be measured and contained—
the government says so. And the world will sail
over the carbon peak: we'll be in free fall
the whole sweet way to paradise regained.

It's slow, of course. The children want to burn
anything that burns. They say we stole
the magic brand, and scraped the sun's wheel
to light it, so shut up: it's their turn
to hit the gas, tank up, ignore the brakes,
as children should. *Just let us be children,*
they wail from blazing consoles. And we tell them,
or try to, what it was to drive that borrowed
chariot, rocketing, spiralling with its florid
machinery in a thunder of gold tyres
down, down the yellowing sky-waste. *Oh infelix*
Phaethon, earth grew nothing then, but fires.
We drove death into childhood, just being children.

DIG

That asphalt strip, gritty raw pink which flanks
The central reservation's monorail
Became their last resort, its narrow strand
The only place where anxious human walking
Could happen, *in extremis*. Trivial flotsam
Laps at the drainage grids: strange coins of soil,
Some bat-like thing—a biker's rotted glove?—
Dust-heaps the forests shed for dearth of leafage
And a white tissue-ball with one torn wing
Beating, flittering in the wind. Why bother
Examining this evidence of pathos,
Scrunched shyly like a precious human secret?
Whether it's food or make-up, blood or shit,
Can't matter if there's no-one's name on it.

ITINERARY

Quickly we move on our chain of moving selves
Though the journey we always remember has taken years:
We stopped at the stations, got out, strolled up and down,
Learnt voices, prices, hand-shakes, fluently settled
Into the customs, unique, yet lords of the local.
These ports and streets we remember by name—our name,
Yet we never touched their ground, never left the moving vehicle

EAST ENDING

For Becky and Roly, and for Wilton's Music Hall

Cable Street, Tower Hill,
East Smithfield, Royal Mint: the traffic sighs
The pointless names, their claimed metonymies,
Blitzed, fragmented, sold remixed and full
of life-forms in suspension.
We hate and love this torpor of museums.

Hate it, mostly. There are stones less rare,
Readable narratives
Threading, sprawling like a London bus queue—
That crush of cultural idioms in one stare.
The cagmag little factories, postcode new,
Pay rent, give birth, live lives.

Yes, *real lives*. Lilacs out of dead money—
The terrace's mild *amour*
Propre of vases, lamps, wives who *salaam*
On steps to shine that cockney dream of Sunny-
Side-of-the-Street, sure as the Sally Army
Bawled in the gin shop, 'Don't have any more!'

History? It's the writing on the walls
Of pubs, a fish bar called The Codfather;
The inn we don't go in, The Artful Dodger;
The DLR train tracks it, and it falls
With shit and feathers from the clattering bridge;
It's seven white skullcaps crossing at the zebra

Towards (we notice now) a mosque's small tower,
So easy in its nook,
It might have jostled longer than St Paul's
Among the brass neck palaces and powers
And leisure craft. Will someone list our malls
One day, finding some pleasure in a look

That thinks itself sheer function, —and improve
The grade 2 concrete with new polymers?
What's the true art of architects? To make it
New, to stitch the shoe we ought to fit?
Let them reinvent the shadowbook—
Not Stilnovisti but New Formalist!

We turn the corner into Ensign Street
Where the best brothels were, and the best turns,
And, prettily distressed as Daisy Bell,
She begs our custom—Wilton's Music Hall.
Her fragile balcony's a work in progress.
Be careful! She's fresh bathed and tremulous,

Her tits like pearly scandals and her ankles
Barley sugar. To restore the old,
Make old just new enough not to disturb
The ghost of Champagne Charley and his girls
Backstage. It's kitsch. So what? So's Shakespeare's Globe.
An audience works the glitz until it's gold.

Word perfect, we belt out those choruses
Oh, don't have any more, Mrs. Moore!
And fill the wormy hollows with our noise
Or you won't find your front door, Mrs. Moore!
Our mobiles wink from gallery to pit,
To catch the past, show us ourselves in it.

SUNSET FOR THE UNDER FIVES

At first, it seems merely surprising, aberrant:
Grandpa, sailing the sunset beyond his pipe-smoke,
Grandma in rolled-down stockings, wandering off to play
And losing her marbles somewhere—a laugh-less adult joke.
We get it slowly. It happens not only to quaint
Creased folk, born long before us, this curious jaunt,
And sunset is not what they see, but the hard earth's turning away.

MUST HAVE

If not the person—
Their stuff.
Diamonds.
Windchimes.
Paperweights.
Watches.
Freezer-ready soul-food.
Give us the ash.
We'll do the animation.

CONVERSATION

Without hearing, I learned to listen to you.

I learned, without a body, to make love to you.

I heard you faintly, worded your snarls or smiles,
The smell of your mood.

Sometimes, I'd imagine my hand moving
Over the parts you couldn't bear me to touch—
As idly, lightly, as I touch these lines.

Poems are born with little sign of pressure
And could be removed or lost with even less.

I tell them to speak to me about you. Never
Were poems anything more—except at first
When I hoped there'd be a reader to believe them.

Without reading, I learned to listen to you.
Believed, without any body, what it was to be loved.

ENGLYNION, BANGOR PIER

I walk across the pearl-grey Menai Strait.
Then I wait at the pier's end,
Watching the broad ripples fanned

By a boat, one sea-mew swimming.
Through dimming light, as I turn—
Snow-bright Snowdon, a thin moon.

from **Animal People** (2016)

ON THE SPECTRUM

*

You look back at your life, or up. It's a winter night
clear-skied. One constellation figures bright
and nameable, and makes the darkness right:

the constellation Art (or Maths or Science or
Loveable Eccentricity, if that's what you prefer).
It's the articulation of the best of what you were.

You pull the sharp-edged stars into a fat bouquet;
you know the gods are idiots, but, being human, pray.
You tell the children, These are roses. What else can you say?

You look back at your life, or up. The moonless sky's
old book of knowledge is a research exercise
where experts thoroughly expose your expertise.

You're wrongly psyched, sad poet! See, the dark's unsigned—
no glittering sword and belt; your metaphors, slipped rind,
one twisted-metal star-collision mirroring your mind.

*

No more the one-letter pronoun   no more the tricks of your verb-
    trade
all is intransitive only   the child picks asphodel

Never your fingers quick on the obsolete harp   and the torches
flowing in amber streams   over the days   gone out.

What is retrieved or remembered? Have you a jar for the fountain?
Have you a small enough jar   for the ash of your being ?

*

Much is misplaced as shadows cross the white light of the temple.
        Dismantle
the neurones, God. Then try to find your image.

*

A kids' party is foreign languages
screamed at you as she as you as he as you run about the little island
no boats are visiting for the next thousand years

*

Tired. Say that. She was tired
or say she tried

tried it and tired it for sixty years   tried it on
till a moment ago, a quarter to
                                        now
tried to edit it all to all right   all righted   again a
gain   We ride it   till twenty past trying   till
the final date with

*

Sleep. my little almond, my little nut-case

and rest   ever-unknowing
not even a moth-mouth chasing you
not your own thumb
                              testing you   inch-worm   petal.
Sleep, little Neanderthal

No species learns from dying how to do
death well   not even Brother Human

*

On the bomb-site there was a fox
stretched mid-leap   the leap made sleep   un-muscled
in the quick blue fly-light

I was afraid of words that bled   but I could look at death
kindly, and keep its fur-shred   knowing it little as love

*

How does those girls know the same secret and say it
how are their sharing without it words or why
is the hair so bright and pale and what are they laughing?

*

You know, of course, not to make the being-sick face
if They have sausages roping out of their nose, not to laugh if They
are eating tissue-paper from space-blue hands

not to screw your finger, snigger the scare-word *mad*
although They are, because they're a Mongol Child
(Are you catching their mustn't-say madness?)

You know when someone cries, like your arm's afraid of their
        shoulder,
like your skin shrunk   you go hollow-sick and grey –
crybaby sobs – you don't know who. Is it *You,* like*?* Or, like, *They?*

*

I listed all the pieces, with all their Köchel numbers,
and listened to them all, eventually.
I got to know the 212 emotions
as well as Mozart knew them -
the tiniest modulations, the accidentals,
which keys might tell a girl love'   and make her wet
despite the ink on her lips, the notes all over her fingers.

*

She a mask, a gash, a lapse, a chromium hasp.
She paintstrips you with her pashes, her clasps soon grasp.
Her aspie-friends frisk with her (gasp!) on the ticklish cusp.
Her jam's a stash, her sleep a wisp. Her dance beats brass.
She's Pandora's whirling cache: adze jigger axe saw screwdriver
    rasp.

*

AM: Aliens Onset.
In a seat, solemn,
ET's animal-nose
Emails a sonnet:
'Am I a stone lens?'

Male-ant noises.
I'm sanest alone
Online at a mass -
O silent as amen.
'I am a stone lens.'

*

If we had friends, we'd think
fifty years without a word essential

If we had money
there'd be days we'd blow the lot on party selves.

*

Over your little lives like the bodies of birds,
I called the winds of my love-and-art affairs
to scatter leaves, sweet leaves,
and apples and new handkerchiefs.

It was Autumn though I didn't know it
because the wind smelled kind
and the dry leaves smelled of life,
and you weren't dead at all, but running, untouched,
towards your indestructible horizon.

I see you now for the last time, sentinel
in the iron branches over the iron bedstead
where I lie as I always lay,
solitary, naked, trying
to be covered by a wind of green kisses.

*

There could never have been a lover—
my love is not fitting.

Nor a child for my Poundland cradle—
my love is not fitting.

Nor a mother-and-father for my Judas kiss.
They had True Love. My love was never fitting.

But when I pray, is there nothing
unborn enough, unasking,

unseeing enough, enough
away to want no small-talk?

If it has heard of itself
it hears no news of our damage.

It is the Unbeloved:
the truth we have never failed,
who makest us also immeasurable.

Who art within our syndrome.

Note: **On the Spectrum**

The final sequence of this collection, 'On the Spectrum,' explores from a female perspective some of the effects and affects of Autistic Spectrum Condition (ASC). My purpose was to present vignettes of a woman's life, partly my own, as poetic documentary. Current research has found evidence of gender differentiation in the way the condition presents, but many more studies will be needed in order fully to understand autism in females. In the meantime, women on the spectrum are often stereotyped according to the diagnostic criteria of male autism – which may also be stereotypical. Personal testimony—even a poet's—has a place in enlarging the view.

Autism may be associated with genes which have been passed down through the intermarriage of Homo Sapiens and Neanderthal Man, and originate from the genetic make-up of the latter. The variant gene DRD47K is thought to be implicated. There is some evidence that AS individuals, male and female, have an unusual affinity with animals, and, judging from the behaviour of my family and friends 'on the spectrum,' I find this credible. For people so often embarrassed by mis-communication, and stigmatised by the kwikfit attributions of literal-mindedness and want of empathy, the notion of an ability to form special cross-species relationships is certainly an attractive one.

We're all animal people in the broader sense, of course: as Bertholt Brecht wrote:

I'm friendly to people. I put on
A stiff hat like they do.
I say: they're animals with a quite particular smell.
And I say: it doesn't matter, I am too.
('Of Poor Old B.B.' Tr. Peter Lach-Newinsky)

'Autistic individuals with a narrow focus of interest and a high capacity for technical thinking and pattern recognition would easily filter into specialized roles in the technological and natural realms as their gifts would make them inventors of technology, keen observers of pattern in weather and in animal behavior, as well as star gazers and calendar makers. The rigid and analytical thinking of such people could lead to the breakthroughs in human behaviors which reduced resource stress and increased longevity, ultimately leading to population increase. Indeed, such thinking could be taught to others who themselves were not autistic yet were perfectly capable of following a standardized method of observation and behavior.' ('Autism, the integration of "difference" and the origins of modern human behavior.' P. Spikins, Cambridge Archaeological Journal, 2009).

'Neanderthals were the original rebel rock-stars.' Garret LoPorto, *Huffington Post* blog, 27.2.12.

AN ARTISTIC FAMILY

We were girl-wives with an idea of beauty so simple
it featured cushions and coffee-mugs, and, once,

the matching of wallpaper to high aspiration—
a frieze. On bands of coarse cord-trim she pearled

French knots—pale green on blue, maroon on grey; she plotted
hearth-rugs in black-and-white geometries famous

as Modern Art. I favoured stripped-pine floorboards,
clashed with acrylics; she preferred Axminster's

Turkey-red with the dark-oak Jacobean
of nineteen-thirties marriage. Both of us relished

the irony of Woolworth's 'wrought-iron' planters.
She liked to quote what a teacher said about her:

'She'll have a beautiful home. She's so *artistic*.'
The beauty we could buy was decoration's

trivia, and we laughed about that, too.
'If you want a beautiful home, marry a wealthy man.'

Neither of us did, but we went on being artistic.
I see it, more and more often,

and farther back:—the drip of Liquid Lino
on the beaks and wings of her customised Flying Ducks,

the squirrel buttons, blue, for a girl's first cardie,
and the delicate green-and-gold Greek-key design

of our famous frieze, the best in the Wallpaper Book,
lifting the child-long day in her tiny dining-room.

EASTER SNOW

'There was a man of double deed
Sowed his garden full of seed...'

Anon.

'And so I've found my native country...

Attila József

There was a man of double deed
Sowed his garden full of snow,
Lit a stove he could not feed,
Sired a child he could not grow,
Who fashioned birds from wooden blocks,
And when their wings fused flight to dark,
And when the dark swept through the locks,
Fetched a book and made an ark.
But who could sail so deep a ship,
Or marry beast to bolting beast,
Dance as he would his flimsy whip
Over the backs of the deceased?

Poets must tell the truth, you said:
The poor must, too, although they lie.
We listen at your iron bed,
Under the tunnel of the sky,
And ask you softly what you need—
Blue roller-skates? A football team?
But you are far and far indeed.
And all the stumbling magi bring
Is the smoke-haze of a dream,
A floating girl, a greasy bear,
A courtyard echo-echoing
The snowy wing-beats of your heart
Towards the deficit of air—
Predicted in your natal chart.

THE TEACHER AND THE GHOSTS

(after *A Christmas Carol,* Charles Dickens)

There were two, a boy and a girl.
He tried to say they were fine children
but the words choked. *A lie of such magnitude.*

This boy is Ignorance. This girl is Want.
He sat up, startled. The room was itself, bright;
the time on his wrist as it should be.

Boxing-Day trade outside. Girls and boys
in their smart affordable brands,
shopping, texting, playing; time

on their side. *Beware them both and all*
of their degree but most of all beware
this boy. He shook off the lie. They were fine children.

SPRING FORWARD, FALL BACK: A GWYNEDD SKEIN

milk-tooth   eirlys
an earth-cub's yawn

soaked his black fur
beneath iâ du

frost on our ffos
                        by noon
                                      frogspawn

*

field-alchemy   manichaean
    miaren   girlfights
harts-tongues and horse-tails
   in the green ash-grove
grasshopper   doorbells

*

          slow grass horse
     gwinau march
fall-back pegasus
    bear our particulate
       wherever birches ride
          branchy in the blue

*

first on the moon
on the bare draen du
a single redstart

the day I leave
let clouds cancel
          the looking-back   these
                                                  mountains

Spring Forward, Fall Back – mnemonic for BST clock-adjustments.
Cymraeg: eirlys – snowdrop, iâ du—black ice, ffos— ditch, miaren—brambles, grinau march— chestnut horse
draen du – blackthorn

THE HOMELESS SHIP *(seen from the Bangor-Chester train)*

Coastline of caravans, neat as graves, but quieter,
rank on rank of them, with a permanent way
like a peace line slicing through: inscrutable classifications—

boundaries, properties, origins.
Washed-out-tired of looking across a too-
small sea, we blank the peninsular horizon.

A factory drops dead leaves, the land reverts to grazing,
and there's our ship, beached, ruminant, rusting.
It fell in love with the wrong colour of pastoral,

and now it waits for a tide that never comes near,
bleak as the child in the inland caravan,
or an emigrant, detained. His palms and shins

skinned to a roar of salt, he's delirious,
surfing the lorries night after night, believing
this is the night he'll cross the sea to England.

MARCH MORNING, PEARSON PARK (for Maurice Ruherford)

Victoria, so young, so white, so modern
for 1854, seems reassured:
the people in the People's Park deserve her,
and, revels quarantined by calico
and carriage-drive, have earned their prophylactic –
beef, beer and Madame Genevieve's rope-trick.
'The foot is free-er, and the spirits more
buoyant when treading the turf than the harsh gravel'
said Zachariah Pearson, speculator,
bankrupt shipper and philanthropist,
who squared things with his conscience, on reflection,
bath-chaired beside the unattractive lake.

In early spring the trees' wrung hands implore
winter to stop it; the forsythia's tiny
oilskins drip, and the bedding-plants are sat
in rows in railed-off, graveyard rectangles,
dim-eyed as board-school children. If they blossom—
a primula here, a dwarf iris there—
the only colour's royal, unreal purple.
Two teenagers beside the listed fountain
play some new kind of netless badminton.
The bright white fantail of their shuttlecock
takes off, lands, takes off, its flight-path slow
as slo-mo through the February-ish air.

LUMEN DE LUMINE (AFTER EDGAR BUNDY'S 'THE NIGHT SCHOOL')

His pillar of Biblical gold
is leaking height,
its tallow hollowing out
like faith in a too-industrious
lily-of-the-field.

He's making notes on oxygen and light,
and that stor thing
where Workers of the World Unite,

fired-up, though hope's all nesh and scant.
Is there a thorny crown
in this religion? Or a bended knee?

Sometimes, it's like he's been laid off again,
to yell and scuffle on the quay,
wild with an agony of entitlement.

Yorkshire words:
Nowt - nothing
Stor – great
Nesh - cold

TWO BIRTHDAY CARDS

1 Under Moel Rhiwen

Sam, 6

Your sky, my sky
seem the same—
smoke-drifts, pearls,
feathers of snow.

The years stream
their weather. Yours
are bare new hills.

Climb. Climb slow

2 White Night

Yura, 80.

Peach without a stone—
dense silver flesh
faintly ashen.

This night's almost
other-night taste;
dawn-dry sleep-thirst.

Warm. No shadow.
Voices and dew-fall
of Letnyi Sad.

Your half-clear face
in the small darkness—
summer's lease.

PRAYING WITH THE IMAM AT SUMMERFADE

Willow herb   jasmine   convolvulus   wild roses
We know what America brings us,
the Imam sings, *America brings us roses*
And Europe flings us jasmine.
We know what flowers they bring us.

I'm ashamed I can bring so little—
only this old Welsh text, illuminated
white and red, earth's litany, autumn-muted.
The shiny, weak, bright-stemmed convolvulus
spirals round the stalks of the rose-bay willow.

And they forge the usual wild embrace, the swaying
deadlock of equals, yet
both are in flower; the day's sufficiency feeds them.
Bees are scarfed in gold   the goldfinch misted silver

willow herb   roses   jasmine   convolvulus   pray for us
ac yn aur ein hangeu.

Cymraeg: *ac yn aur ein hangeu – now and at the hour of our death* (from the *Ave Maria*).

HAPPY SEVENTIETH BIRTHDAY BLUES, MR ZIMMERMAN

I'm staring into seventy, staring at that old bad news,
Yeah, staring into seventy, staring at the rank bad news.
I'm getting slowly smashed, but it's not the getting smashed you'd choose.

It's a wall that's got no garden shining on the other side,
A wall that's got no pardon, smiling on the other side –
Just ask any angel who ever crossed that divide.

I heard the devil singing, he was singing to me long ago,
He sang me through the sixties, he sang me years and years ago –
Sang *Man, if you're a woman you just have to grow and grow.*

I'm a long-born woman, and it's the shortest straw.
I'm a long-born woman, smoking my cheroot of straw.
But I'm no damned angel, I was born to be a whole lot more.

I'm looking at the wall. Are you telling me it's a gate?
I'm looking at a wall, yeah, he's telling me it's the gate.
You can find it if you're blind, baby blue, it's not too late.

We're only ever twenty, we're only ever at the start.
We're only ever peddling that iconic parabolic start.
And there's no wall, baby, it's the shadow of an empty heart.

Go cruising into seventy: seventy's a broad highway;
Cruise along at seventy, along that broad highway –
You'll soon be doing eighty, if the angels get out the way.

ALL SOULS' SATURDAY NIGHT

In the corner of my living-room, she'll sit
watching herself on TV
lost in a vision of mobility
which doesn't hurt, or almost doesn't hurt—

they said I was cut out to be a dancer.

Foxtrot, waltz, tango, samba, rumba—
the glitter-balls revolve:
a ghost of taffeta holds her, slips her on—

doctors should kill us off when we get to sixty.

She swims the air
with swollen broken-slippered feet; her see-through
hands drift to unlock
the rack of hips: she stands, she's twisting free
in the shudder of a beginner's paso doblé,

and steps out partnerless – who needs a man
to kick-in the glass, glissade into a streaming
of stars across space-time to be
her own blue heaven? There's the empty chair—

you should have seen me at the Hippodrome

and in my living-room, her quick-step quickens,
lightest, brightest among them, and the glance
over her shoulder knows I'm watching her
somewhere, on television.

JOHN RODKER COMPOSES A COLD ELEGY FOR ISAAC ROSENBERG

no more will that pronoun in your sealed hand
nor the tricks of your verb-wires   trip me

no more shall the brush-fire   you sowed   fanned
                                        sweep by & gut my   dirt-
    town

  flirt on   whip of stars   red heap
        alas my lipless!
              see
your miraculum   your misillery   crackle   into closedown

PYRAMID TEXT

When the king wants the war,
The soldier wants the war.
When the soldier wants the war as the king wants it,
The war loves the soldier.
When the soldier wants the war as the king wants it,
War loves the kingly soldier and the king's god loves him.
The army shines from the south, its swelling river
Spreads glittering sky all over the hard fields.
The soldier shines from the south, he wants the kingdom
As the swelling river wants it, spreads his glittering torrent
Over the rocks and drenches the hard fields
With sky, and scatters stars of grain: when the soldier
Wants to become the seed, the soldier sows the kingdom
In corn so tall it reaches the king's shoulders
And bends its ears as he whispers
Bring me the bread of war. Bring me the soldier.

ZOOTOCA VIVIPARA

The lizard taketh hold with her hands
and she is in kings' palaces,

the spectacle of her accomplished
evolution a tiny
fragment of bronze-blue mosaic
after an explosion,

her species older than the birds,
and closer to the stars
that are still very close, and molten
behind their rays,

a juvenile *vivipara,*
her fore-hands lifted
in a last, eloquent gesture,

who touched the Permian desert
and the Anthropocene,
where she sticks, flat as a stamp,
in her new little suit of lights.

SONG OF THE OBSOLETE

Once there was much to be made, much to be made, much to be made,
Much to be sold to be sold to be sold;
Much to mix, mash, mould, much to split, splice, spoil, much to catch, much to carr
    And you in the mills and mines and millinery rooms
Was small as a coal and twisted
And cheap as a lie but the labour
Was bread and you kept at it kept at it kept
At your keep, your bare keep, the bare earnings you'd barely keep.

Now what's to make, mister? Sister, what'll you sell?
You hated us didn't you hated us didn't you hated
The handles you heaved, the treadles you waded, the windlass that wound you.
    But now where's the hoist for your hope?
Where's the job, the five bob, the slick rob, the quick sob, and the picketline's glory?
    Don't look at us don't look at us don't look at us.
We'd give you the works if we worked. We don't work. End of story.

Where are the bastards that built us, the slavers that skilled us -
The pay-packet packer, the docker with dockets, the stacker of profits, the stockist?
What are our hours, now it's time that maims and mills us?

HOME THOUGHTS FROM THE COW-SHED (FOR YURA)

When streets and signs reclaimed Cymraeg, our pad
spat out its Saxon—Pinfold—and became
Buarth Gwarchau (native speakers say 'Bith Gwar-kai.')
Both names had lustre, but the hard-to-tame
Welsh was the one to brag about with friends—
English friends. *It's cow shed, cattle yard.*
So it suits us! And so it strangely did.

Sinking, weathering, stiffening, wind-erupting
like *gwartheg* ghosts, we settled for the subtle
exchange of birch-tree and boletus, grass
and flesh. The farm dissolved into its sideline
of caravans, but when we lived here first,
March brought, along with daffodils, the fine,
black, yellow-tagged bull-yearlings, and their lust.
They'd snort and shove and tear the gorse; at night-time,
stand quietly in the ditch, and look at us.

The farmer up the road has plans to graze
two horses in their empty field. He patches
the fence with crates. The hawkweed will be sowing
new stars, and harebell sky will frame our riches
a little longer. Both of us were blow-ins
but you, by dying here, became a native—
(although you never learned to say 'Bith Gwar-kai').
I'll find some new *boleti* where the birches

and fungus share their sugars of decay,
remembering with what care you'd delve your pen-knife,
so that the spores might fruit another day.

Cymraeg – the Welsh language
Gwartheg – cattle

DANAE, DINARII

'As wolves love lambs, so lovers love their loves"
(Phaedrus, Socrates*)*

The pursuit of Immortality, bragged the Poet,
was nothing! I was young
and showered with starry faces.

Not divinities, he said—these were people:
boys, girls, much alike—just people—
the same lizard brains, the same jack-hearts,

the same unbeatable-value profiles, lips
shopping around for kisses.

They've crumpled now, he said. They smiled too much, got scaly
or soft. But the originals,
pocketed at the moment

the mouth my own had touched
sang from the fire, are hard and fine and sovereign.
Savings, he grinned. *Poets' currency.*

IT'S TIME FOR THE WEATHER!

Blizzle lightens to *waterbud* before strengthening to *pluvoria*
& *seaflay* later *smogmer* steadily thickening to *notabretha*
summerlonglast is *fade* becoming *saturbang*
bangfrice brings plummeting temperatures
the outlook's *katabase,* followed by rising *hellglow humitude*
and a *dowly* prospect
of *glumtideyule*
buy your solar credits now if you're worried about
allyeargridoffswindlemas
Enjoy the rest of your evening!!!

HAPPY CHRISTMAS, SISTER DYMPNA

'Animals *are* people!' Sister Dympna feeds the camera
that twinkly look she got through being chosen
from all the whining, wagging, weaving strays in the enclosure
to be Love's Guide-Dog and the Nation's Anchor.
She can't keep cats. Or terrapins. They're people
and she's reserved for God. A venial sin, you say,
this heresy, but what does Pope Francis say?
Has God agreed to a new species-steeple?

Animals don't have souls. Horns, hooves, et cetera,
aren't suited to the sacred menagerie.
No pets, no God, I thought. I had a hamster
I loved and taught some tricks and challenges,
claiming her (airborne in a basket) First
Hamster into Space. And when she died
(in bed and full of hamster-years) I cried.
I'd been a little beast; my skin was fur, reversed.

In those days, mice could sew, dogs dance, and fuchsia piglets
with hats and ginghamed picnic-tables perved
our childhood dream of childhood. Animaddictive,
Tom was an evil psycho, and deserved
to be cat-pancakes. Dragons, less than furry,
grinned *ranckes of yron teethe*, burned fossil fuel, and crunched
Anglicans, till we charmed them. Then, like us, they lunched
on salad, muttering 'Hurry, oysters, hurry!'

Sister Dympna prays for the word-lords who engrave
small discs with 'Dots-Toyevsky', 'Mopsy-Mow'
or 'Prince.' In her new series, *Boss and Slave*

(the Christmas special, *Hoping it Might Be So*),
she steals the keys to all the Pets-at-Home
cages, and – is she dreaming? – whispers, ‘Run,’
before she kneels, on cue, and finds the new-born Son
curled in his hay, blind as a kitten, bless Him.

SMALL FACTS

The cold snap holds—
  hardly a flicker of wing,
  or sprinkled seed of song.
Cars on the narrowed hill
  are slow and few.
All creatures hide or die
  from snow…

  It blazes at the door
  with a gaze to crack
thin glazing, bricks un- braced
  for zero—but not you.
This severer takes no part
  in your heart-lessened pace,
your sightless turn towards
  the mystery-journey's
imminence… What journey?

And when—(still warm—but when)—
  you're filled with cold,
out in your unprotected
  bed, where earth is heaped
in scarp and fold,
  I'll know not to mistake
the mottling grass or clear
glitter of song or wing,
  for some molecular soul—
what's soul?—re-entering
    earth's atmosphere.

Fact: I shall not re-make
  my snow-man beliefs,
  nor think it consolation
ever that you—or any
  creature in its un-making—
 'quietly'   'sleeps.'

MARSHALSEA QUADRILLE

1.
Debts stacked up like bricks,
at the Tabard as I lay,
watching a chink of sky
from the slushy sticks

the Surrey side of the Thames.
Debts stacked up like bricks,
and sundry heretics
and smugglers came to terms

but the pauper's room cost double
when the gaoler threw a six.
Debts stacked up like bricks,
the bricks stacked up like trouble

and toppled on the pricks
who'd have chucked them back (fair's fair)
if they'd not been starving where
debts stacked up like bricks.

2.
At the Tabard as I lay,
saving for my salvation,
the criminal population
tripled in a day.

I counted out my cash
at the Tabard as I lay
and then it rolled away.
I heard a distant splash,

but, loaded, didn't care
what load I couldn't pay
at the Tabard as I lay
and prayed some good soul there

would buy my round-e-lay,
and underneath the tap
would thrust his little cap
at the Tabard as I lay.

3.
Watching a chink of sky
he passes Nancy's Stairs,
not knowing they'll be hers -
only that good souls die

un-saved by gilded towers,
watching a chink of sky.
He gulps a ha'penny pie
with a few fanciful tears.

Some grubby gargoyles that
might be debating why
watching a chink of sky
concerns this sewer-rat

jeer as he scuttles by.
To Lant Street, then, and home -
contented in the gloom,
watching a chink of sky.

4.
From the slushy sticks,
a London Particular
snuffs Perpendicular
to smoking wicks.

He often walks all night.
from the slushy sticks,
to skin his cicatrix,
his blister-pack of light,

and save the child who drowned
although he'd learned some tricks
from the slushy sticks –
the child who won't be found

by any politics
or power that snivels pity,
but never walked to the city
from the slushy sticks.

HAMLET (freely after Boris Pasternak)

The noise died. I stepped onto the stage.
And now I lean against a door-frame, tense,
Keyed up for cues, the mutterings of events
Rehearsing the performance of the age.

The deepening dusk's thousand binoculars
Take aim at me, point-blank along the one
Axis. Not a blink. If it can be done,
Father, Abba, I beg—*let my cup pass.*

I love your bloody plots, I'd willingly
Take any part you offered, except this—
The part you're writing now. The scenes unfold

As planned, the actors strut their entrances.
And I'm alone, crushed by the Pharisee.
'To live a life is not to cross a field.'

THREE FADO (freely, from the Portuguese)

1.
There was a sadness
lit up the city.
Not one person
returned my gaze.

Maybe I dreamed it –
a gate flown open,
iris to iris
one blue gaze.

2.
Among deceitful shadows
When far-off stars were breaking,
We gave each other roses
To forget we ever gave them.

To forget we ever gave them
We gave each other shadows
When far off stars were breaking
Among deceitful roses.

Gypsies, green young gypsies,
Give us that song again –
Sins are boys of twenty:
Regrets are deaf old men.

3.
You that wash clothes in the river,
You that chop planks with machetes,

Cutting my coffin to size—
There are rich boys who'd save you;
Buy up the land God gave you,
But your life, nobody buys.

At the round table, singing
We drank from the bowl that circled
With covert kisses and wine.
You gave me water and berries.
You shared your feast, but the bread
Of your life, nobody buys.

I sleep in the simplest bed,
Pressing my cheek to the mud,
Heather and bracken my blanket.
I lie where poverty lies,
And you bless the rich boy with sweet incense,
But forgiveness, nobody buys.

You that wash clothes in the river,
You that chop planks with machetes,
Cutting my coffin to size—
Some say money will save you;
But I have a life to give you,
The life nobody buys.

LAUNDRY BLUE

(freely, after Attila József)

The creaky, loaded basket at her hip,
Mum took the wash up to the drying-attic
and I, a poet even then, stayed back
to stamp around, and make my feelings known.

My howls meant, 'Mum, don't leave me on my own.
Don't hug those babies when you should be hugging
me!' Mum didn't take the slightest notice.
She went on lifting, stooping, reaching, pegging
sheet after glistening sheet, slip upon slip,
darned socks, gradated nurseries of the headless,
and dancing shirts. That's how poor women love -
with pegged lips and an ounce of indigo.

The wet shades still flit and flap above.
I try to rub my tears off, to compose
my roaring face, and…
But Mum can't hold me now. Her grey hair blows
across a sky of rain she's mixed with blue.

THE HARE AND THE HEDGEHOG (after 'Der Hase und der Igel,' *Children's and Household Tales,* Brothers Grimm, 1857)

Who will bury the hare,
the hare left bleeding by the hedgehog's cheating?

He and the hedgehog raced down the field. The hare
was ahead, had almost won when he heard
the shout, 'I'm already here.'
He ran back up like a whirlwind,
Heard 'I'm already here.' Ran down. 'I'm already here.'
Ran up.'I'm already here.'
Need I go on? Need I go on?
But he went on, the hare.

Thirty times, forty, fifty…
He's tired, and the tiredness comes
from a new planet of tiredness,
but his head, full of blood-pump and wildness,
can't work anything out,
can't get at an obvious question
like, Why is that hedgehog so fast
on his laughable trit-trot legs?
Or, Is there another hedgehog in this field?
(as there was, a Mrs. Hedgehog).

Fifty times, sixty times, seventy, seventy-
one, seventy-two, seventy-three…

He was crazy, of course, this hare –
so fast on his one-track feet, so sharply sure,
even flaked out, blood leaping
from ears and eyes and the curled-back lips, brain spinning,
he laughed with his hare-self, winning.

The hedgehogs snorted and grabbed
the prize—one coin and some brandy—
like the swindling peasants they were.

And the heart-broken, beautiful hare
seethes in the nettles and sun, melts in the rain and the root-work,
until you can say, Oh, sure—
this is a story. There was never a hare.

Bezdelki

(New, Unpublished Poems)

from *Bezdelki* (The Emma Press, 2017)

'WHEN PSYCHE-LIFE FOLLOWS PERSEPHONE...'

When, through translucent forest, Psyche-life
follows Persephone down into the dark,
a sightless swallow flings itself in her path,
with angry tenderness, and a twig in leaf.

The shades rush round to greet the visitor.
They cry their miseries to a newfound friend,
and wring their feeble hands in bewilderment
and timid longing, stretching out to her.

One offers her a mirror, one, a phial of scent.
The soul's a woman, you know, these small things matter.
Over the sterile woods, their voices patter
like dry raindrops, equally transparent.

The soul's confused by all this tender fussing.
The glassy oaks, she thinks, must be a dream;
she breathes onto the mirror, takes her time
fumbling out her coin for the misty crossing.

BEZDELKI, WITH MORPHINE

I don't know what you dreamt of—your first fuck
or the last teaspoon-sip of strawberry yoghurt?
Perhaps you poked an earthbound walking stick
at some enchanting 'find,' some tiny engine-part?

Your breath came fast and steadily; when less
than audible, I thought it only sleep's
new, uneventful phase. Later, I fetched the glass
and held it to your mouth. I kissed your lips

and felt, this time, no little answering pull,
the reflex of reflection, two as one.
(Don't worry: shades, you know, are kissable.)
I woke my phone. The compact's swing-glass shone.

I don't know in what currency you paid,
or if you saw the leafless crystal oaks,
or if a mist came down, or a mist cleared,
as the ferryman and you exchanged small jokes...

Thus Psyche-life, who studied animation
at a fine film-school, storyboards the sequel,
a short montage for the remotest reel
far beyond metaphor and adaptation.

She's your material girl: there's lots to do.
She finishes the yogurt, washes spoons
and sheets, dusts mirrors, picks up small possessions
like clouds, and watches them turn into you.

SUMMER VISITOR

The little boy found him on the couch.
He was a distant relative, maybe an uncle's uncle.
His mouth gawped and the air above it sizzled
as *muscae domestica* spread the news
of the fine, moist laying-caves in Uncle Slava.

Their eyes are rouge spots, their embroidered wings
rainbow when the sun forces an entry
through the dacha's webby glass;
the boy gulps and stares and sucks his thumb,
the dead man sighs his millions of girl souls.

VIDUA

I wasn't a bride.
I wasn't a wife.
I'm not a widow.
I'm no one, trying to gather
all the 'we were's together.

Widewe, wuduwe—
two double-yous, one an echo,
one a shadow.

I wear no ring.
I'm not even Akaky Akakievich.
I'm *vidua*, twice. I'm a hole
meeting a hole. I'm two ruined overcoats.

DIASPORA

The toolshed you called your Jewish Box
(cleverly designed and 'Made in Israel')
has been dismantled by northeasterly gales,
its seven, tough, moulded plastic pieces
bullied apart, thrown any old where. I've saved them
but I can't make a house: the walls
are too heavy, the doors won't meet,
relationships with a roof have been broken off.

I round up the soaked ex-residents,
the strimmer, the chipper, the saw, the bucket of wood
ready-chopped for a barbecue,
and the refugees I can't name…
They glisten darkly in the grass,
defiant old metals, coupled
irrefutably and awkwardly for life:
a rake head with wide handlebars,
a giant's steel bracelet bolted to a griddle.

Your artefacts. Laced secretly all over
by the tiny snails of your dreams
and your DNA. But lost in the rain rush
and wind wash, they can't tell me
why they exist, where they want me to shelter them.

I'm not a princess in red stilettos.
I'm a hard-muscled woman,
waterproofed against tears;
unafraid of embracing the dead.
I'm your *zaichik*, the hare that dodged the hunter's

bullets, and skipped home. But I don't know how to build
or mend a house of tools
that are sullen and fierce and have no words without you.

I don't want to weep into a mirror.
I want to check credentials, ask what they're for;
perhaps see a demonstration,
and nod admiringly, and name them.
I'll call them your Russian Tools, or Ukrainian,
or Finnish Tools, or your British Citizen Tools.

I want to gather them in a dry place.
I want you to come and mend the Jewish Box.

RUNNING WITH KING TAHARQA

When the Pharaoh wants the war,
the war wants the Pharaoh.
When the Pharaoh wants the war no longer,
he sinks into the sand, already a sphinx—
and the drum, the drum he hates more than the war drum
(who's banging it so hard, his weightless heart?)
slips away from his chest, devolves to footfall.
*
Dawn. Sole beat and water song.
The river my sister sings the shape of herself,
leaps where the lion leaps, dances past the lion
on his short rope, appetite:
sometimes pretends to do nothing—
marsh-maker, rock-sucker, sky-mirror,
word-weaver, choked with papyrus;
rouses again, and races the lion-man's racing:
foam-fleck, foot-flash, rainbow-flake, two of us neck-and-neck,
slipping past settlements, slopping in rock-pools, black
and white in the crash-sites, slow and snakeskin-yellow
through Memphis into *hundred-gated Thebes.*

The Kushite cub, nosing in the ruins,
felt a hand on his shoulder   found himself kneeling—
bread, beer, oxen, birds, my heart being sweet   cause me
to carry to you anything—

and the same hand opened, slid an arpeggio
of light on the toppled pillars,
and played five words: *carry to me my city.*
*

The unfledged papyrus sighs
for water, twisting its toes
in rusty canopic silt
and the beached skiff prays for a river, for you, Amun-
Amun, who drops, who rises
          when the
                    Pharaoh
                              wants the
                                        war
and when the Pharaoh wants the war no longer,
and sags to his hip bone, prayerless,
his sweet heart sucked by five Assyrian arrows.
*
Souls clatter like wings,
like netted marsh-birds, blind
to everything but their sky.

Was this your lion army
or mine, Esarhaddon?
The dead grin up at our flags.
They belong to no state, no species.

Croak with the broken ibis, Pharaoh. Howl with the solders' wives.
*
When I woke, it was only this world.
Thin waves came in from nowhere, rippling the dunes.
The dead rolled over, *ignes fatui*,
and the moonlit boat appeared, dragging threads of new river.
I felt a hand on my shoulder   felt that muscle
of air in the silk-cool desert night. Amun
(wiser than Xerxes) wanted
it seemed   to call off the war   no longer wanted

a king who wanted a war (or a war that wanted a god).
*
Taharqa, already a sphinx,
moves his eyelids, remembering.
*
At first, we were playing a game. We joked and jostled,
but we knew our race would become
a temple, we felt that darkness.
Soon, with a fiercer beat and concentration,
we ran, just ran ran on ran on and on our lungs
high lyres we scrubbed the burning from our eyes
which filled and burned again the smears of palm trees
were ghosts, we thought, not messengers. And then

the victor crashed the finishing rope, and flung
himself across, and we all
flung ourselves across, broken with laughter
and moaning, lightly wounded pride the same
for slave and king, runner-up and also-ran.

We praised each other, thanked the gods, we plunged
our mouths in bowls of pomegranate wine.
Amun was writing on the broken stelae
of ripples where we skinny dipped, and each
to his own hot floating face said the god's name.

*
By the river that rises in the Otherworld
where everyone's god is his heart, mixing him freshly
from blood and darkness
drumming him upwards
drumming him

to wake to a new forgetting,
I become the scratch of script, the scribe's light reconstruction:

He flung the molten ball Jerusalem
to you, the future. Memphis, he returned
to the gods. He won a kingdom
lovely as waterfalls; he lost a desert.
He liked to run, Taharqa: he ran with his men.

*

Listen. These words are our breathing,
our cloud of silvery spores on glass, our thunder
across packed sand, our fluids on leaf balm and linen,
our pattering sand-grains, blinked from the eyes of heaven.

New Uncollected Poems

THE PERHAPS-BAG

As long as you lived, I carried an *avoska,*
my hope, however glum,
the shops, however haunted.
In every queue, it was the same:
I missed the special offer by a whisker
but found myself presented
with a glut of dead bread-rolls.
I'd rush home, tripping over
the trinkets and lost souls
raining through everyone's sieve,
and light the stove.
I lived for your simple waiting,
(one fragment less of myself),
a joke ('good catch!'), your sudden appetite,
the gleaming which unwraps
fresh bread and fills the shelf,
and every ragged hole of the *perhaps*.

FINGER MARKS

What light is left for our nightfall?
Not even the light of that question,
since one of us is nothing light can enter—
a particle of absence in the spectrum
of absences.
                              So, like a normal couple,
we learn how to caress the intangible,
to name the natures of shadow:
shadows awaited, lovely shade remembered,
shade uncannily clear, shade secretive,
shades appalled and breathless
on the snarled terrace, purgatorio of Heysel.

But the shade in the room with us once—
that room with the sink, the window, the two mountains
so many eyes had flown to -
it was caught by the light, and light
found a person. I touched you in person
three times as you ran fresh water
onto the dishes and said,
almost cheerful (as if describing Moscow),
no, it's not very good there
but I can't come back.

Chè tu se' ombra.
Somewhere I'll find the words, and send you their light
in a leaky parcel—look, I'm still working on it.
These wretched smears, like the fingers of Statius
on dissolving anklebones,
cling to the shoulders of your thick, checked shirt
my daughter's boyfriend, working on the roof,
fills with more slender shoulders.

THE DIALECT

(Remembering Fedya, a Favourite Cat)

Playful, practical, mundane,
One brain, for a littler brain,
Stitched a cap of language. How—
Though your mouth was all Miaow—
Strange that you could catch the phrases
Warning, wheedling, singing praises.
Daft diminutives! Poor few
Vocables invoking you
& me as odd affiliates
In fricatives and affricates.
Old and weak and blind, you lay
In cosy corners, but one day,
Crossed the dreadful road, came back,
Sharper faced and shinier black,
And purred, triumphant to correct
The scold-sound of our dialect.

It was pre-Neanderthal -
Syntax, basic; tone range, small.
No philologist had cried
When, with you, the dialect died,
And the silent speaker left
Doubly, stupidly, bereft,
Typed out rhymes to shame and bore
The clever stuff most words are for.

SWEET THINGS

1. *A Boiled Sweet*

That little sugar-free fruit drop
I found in your overcoat pocket—
can't eat it,
can't stop tasting it.

2. *Choceur*

The most reluctant chocolate ever made:
12 bitter squares per bar,
each bar worth 192 calories,
the skinniest lining of marzipan.
Nothing to kiss the tongue, to sweeten tears.
I told you to shop at Waitrose, not at Aldi…

The wrapper is the bright unfaded red
of your old BMW 365
that sat six weeks outside, dulling and ailing
without your hands and feet to prod its memory,
sting it with fuel, fire its lights, and blast it
with Vysotsky's existential, tobacco-black rage.

To you, they were luxury.
those so-called Rich, so-called Marzipan, marvels.
I told you to shop at Waitrose, not at Aldi
but you liked a Special Offer, a Three-for-the-Price-of-One.
It was capitalism's finest.

You hid them from yourself—
your six slim promises with the French name,
too good to break, to taste, too good for the bourgeoisie –
a *sovok*'s dream of *pineapples in champagne.*
Eventually, tenderly, they'd be pieced out
week by week, over the duration
of your body's perfectly organised revolution.

3. *Wild Strawberries*

One month beyond your last birthday
in beds of wild strawberries
that began with one frail plant,

you're living hand to mouth
like the runners and the tiny red fruits.
All cells want to multiply.

Cancer cells are innocent
as strawberry cells, as the fingers
that loosen the strawberries.

4. *Blueberries*

Your last time outside
you walked about thirty paces
to the scrawny blueberry bushes.
You wore your heaviest jacket
and leant on your stick through the mush
of frostless leaves.
A carton on a string
bobbed round your neck.

Once it would have been filled,
but the willows had grown too dense
and the plants were sun starved.
Still, you were proud of your handful
of midnight-blue full moons,
sweeter for being rare.
I pick them too, this year—
a few sun-catching moments
from your last walk out of doors
in your last October.

BLACK RAINBOW

In the evening when
our parent star has stretched
a diagonal chimney stack

over the cooling yard
the cats come by and sit—
four mute soliloquies.

They groom themselves, but not
particularly, share
shiny green glances, wait—

for what? What darker thing?
I dish out food. *Not this,*
their calm bodies tell me—

the moment is the feast;
there may not be another.
Leaves spit and crackle.

The black rainbow shatters
in four swift pieces. Shadow
pours from roof and sky.

NARRATIVE OF SUCCESS

The light was pale, dawn-like. There was a hill and I was watching a stream of girls (mostly girls) dancing and floating over the top of it, and these people were narratives, they were successful narratives, they were short stories and novels which had been chosen for prizes, poems which had brought delight, and works of scholarship which also quietly sang. I watched them with longing: my narrative wasn't there. Then a man and a woman, you and I, found ourselves in a tunnel. It was a London underground tunnel; we were alone at the end of a long narrowing platform, and we were in each other's arms. The man who was you said to me, as if he had seen the hill narratives, too, 'I know how much you wanted your writing to give me good things' and we wept together. For the first time I knew that my own poor narratives were not wasted; if they had told that story to him, they were not, after all, the pure delirium of self-interest, but sometimes useful, kindly acts of love.

THE CLASP

Again, the dream that's not all dream,
but a dream folded back
to smudged awaking, and, again,
that sudden, heavy sensation,
the clumsy, nuanced liveness of your fingers,
your fingers round my own. My gasp,
yearning for pleasure, voiceless,
'Where are you now, where are you?'

This time, you squeezed my hand, a quick answer
not to the question, but some older darkness.

THE CONCHOLOGIST WISHES MORE THINGS MIGHT BE CLOTHED IN SHELL

The hazel tree dies loudest, dropping single
leaves like pain-words, stuttered or expletive,
each torn brown-paper mouth bitterly crumpled.
Nothing's so blood crisp, nothing on the concrete
more like a wounded creature's skittering—
except they're dead—seem dead beyond organic.
If they were seashells, empty protein-coats,
they'd be less lost, however scarred. My hand
would turn them slowly, light would twist inside,
disclose the place, pink-lipped, or satiny
as anti-bedsore sheets, where flesh unfolded.
I'd keep forgetting they had sought asylum
far from their soil, and couldn't drift and sink
as nutriment where coral reefs of hazel
were branching cities, mothering their fullness,
their tensile shimmer in green water-light.
I wish all death were exoskeletal,
a whispering gallery for time, for fury.
I wish the earth were wrapped in something pearl-like.
I wish a dead man might be clothed in shell.

MOMENT

Give me a moment like the one which passed
just now across your life
and which you tried to keep.
Turn its face towards me, white and strange,
impossibly lit up and still lit up
as the power fails in all moments following.

SYRIAN ALGEBRA

I'm a smashed jawbone
from a face attacked by shrapnel

finding out I'm still
hung by a thread to a man—
a man who stares up at the fuzzy light
in the underground hospital

and hears a mask make words

I'm open wide like the dentist's

He works on my hinges my lips
my palate all night in the wreckage
swears he'll get the bloody thing right

I'm trying to tell him—thank you Mr
Algebra

and he smiles he heard me when this
new roar rips through the hinges
smashes us into us out of us

we grope the sticky red paste

he can't find any bones

I can't find any skin.

And what about words? Don't ask.
Our children have opened wide, ready with teeth

FREEDOM'S TWILIGHT (AFTER OSIP MANDELSTAM)

Vote for freedom's twilight, girls and boys,
for the great year's darkening.
Forests of fishnets drop
into the foaming night.
Sun, lift your light
above the people. Judge us.

Vote for the block of uranium
our tender leader weeps
to lift. Vote for Atropos.
Vote for the power of rage.
Our statecraft's floundering.
Time, pity our heartbeat.

We bound their wings and sent
the swallows into battle.
The sun's invisible. Branches
tremble and flail and warble.
The sun's invisible but
the world floats free.

Come on, children, heave
the massive creaking helm until
we turn. The world floats free.
Plough the waves. And tell your tyrants: *even*
locked up in Stygian ice we paid
ten heavens to keep this earth.

THE FIRST-GENERATION STUDENT AND THE SECRET SCHOLAR

A door swung open on the space where
'university' met 'corporation'
in a muted, steely glissando.

I mistook you for somebody else,
nobody else, a stereotype of profit,
and bench-mark, obol-murky, paper-light.

I'm years and years too late
for thinking through the conundrum
though I've learned that scholarly kindness

may be a mask, and that masks may be worn over kindness.
A sycamore green-shades your window when
I remember you: can thoughts translate into leaves?

The campus is always September-fresh, the doors
admit us without a card. We first-years crowd
the hall with our voices, again and again and never

STABAT MATER

Stabat mater dolorosa
Juxta crucem lachrimosa…

The trees are light industry, or running water,
though the wind's no more than a trickle of energy.
The stars are big: my ruined eyes say 'stars!'

What a shortfall the days were,
What vast postmortems made room for.
I see I've begun to be hated: thank goodness it's dark!

No one factored in a wept-for daughter,
her blood hard to wash out as it is to imagine
the mind of someone who's constructing hatred

like they're investing in a market garden,
fish farm or factory: some long flow of product.
A mother and a stuck child are abominations.

Let's not in love or hatred stand like icons.
We give what we can. Those who are the gifted
are sometimes leafless trees wishing the wind could read them.

CANTO XXVII (DANTE, *PURGATORIO*)

It was first light where light's first Creator
  had spilled His blood: time's level scale-pans soared
above the Ebro; noon at the equator

saw Ganges simmering: —thus the fallen world.
  Here, the sun was leaving us. Beyond
the barrier flames, God's happy angel carolled.

The hymn he sang, 'Corde beati mundo,
  made purer by the crystal of his voice,
left our own small voices thick with wonder.

As we came closer, his was grave advice.
  'Holy Souls, you must pass through this fire.
Keep listening as you painfully advance:

'You'll hear the music that you most desire.'
  My hands stretched up, white-knuckling each other.
Bodies like mine were twisting on that pyre.

My good guides turned to me. Virgil, my father,
  murmured, 'Punishment, dear child, is not
death. If you're to die, why did I bother

to help you conquer Geryon? Think of that
  rough ride! I swear these flames could interweave
your hair a thousand years, and you'd meet God unhurt.

'Come. Test them with a corner of your sleeve.'
  I was ashamed, but didn't dare to touch;
Stricken with guilt, but didn't dare to move.

My lack of fortitude perturbed my teacher.
'That wall,' he said, 'Is all that stands between
yourself and Heaven's light—your Beatrice.'

Once, when the fabled mulberry lost her green,
the dying Pyramus raised his head on hearing
Thisbe's name, and found her face. So when

those sounds were uttered, sweet, familiar, searing,
I looked up, knowing all my obstinacy
undone. My master nodded. 'So we're staying?'

He smiled, as if I'd been a child of three,
mollified by an apple. We moved forward—
Virgil first—and Statius, following distantly.

Once in the flames, I gasped, I would have arrowed
into the nearest pool of boiling glass
to cool my skin. My gentle father borrowed

consoling fictions: 'Beatrice's eyes
already shine on us!' We heard again
the angel's guiding voice: it rose and rose,

and we emerged where our ascent began.
'Venite, benedicte Patris mei'
welled from a radiance that outshone the sun.

I had to shade my eyes and look away.
'Hurry, before the west is plunged in darkness!'
I turned, my body blocking the last ray,

to mount that steep stair cut through the crevasse.
A short way up, my shadow disappeared,
And night, we knew, had overtaken us.

Each swiftly chose a step, and made his bed.
Our strength was sapped, if not our willingness.
We were like mountain goats who'd leaped and veered

from ledge to ledge but now, in sheltered grass,
watched by the shepherd leaning on his crook,
would feed and browse. I thought how herdsmen pass

their nights *al fresco*, caring for their flock.
My shepherds lay nearby. Immense bright stars
filled the small sky between the parted rock.

I contemplated them until my gaze
dissolved in sleep—sleep with its curious skill
for revelations which foretell the day's.

The same time as Cytherea's brimming shell
flooded the mountain from the east, I dreamed
about a woman, young and beautiful,

who sang: 'Whoever asks my name, I'm named
Leah. My hands are busy weaving flowers
for necklaces—and yet my sister's charmed

by simple looking. Rachel sits for hours
content with her reflection. So we share
the fruits of action's, and of vision's, powers.'

Day break, with that magnificence of cheer
  well-known to travellers home, whose spirits lift
higher each day to feel their goal so near,

coloured the sky. Night's shadows went adrift
  with my departing dreams, and I awakened
to see my masters had already left.

'That apple, for which many boughs are broken
  by ravenous mortals, will today ensure
that you are sweetly feasted.' I was shaken

by Virgil's promise. With each step, the more
  desire sprang up in me. I seemed to grow
wings; I'd soon be light enough to soar!

The stairs had rushed away, and hung below,
  when Virgil fixed me with his eye, and said,
'My child, I understand I cannot go

beyond this point. How far you've travelled, tried
  by flames that pass, and flame unending! Skill
and insight fitted me to be your guide:

'but now let pleasure take on Virgil's role.
  See the great sun that lights your forehead, see
grasses and trees and flowers in the rich soil

'of infinite blooming. You're at liberty,
  after your long, hard climb, to be delighted,
until the lovely eyes, which summoned me,

‘and by whose tearfulness I was conscripted
 into your service, come to you again,
shining with happiness restored, completed.

‘From me, expect no further word or sign.
 Stand tall and free: your will is now your own.
 Trust it, as I trust you. I now assign
to your self-governance, the mitre and the crown.’

A KANDINSKY WOODCUT

Childishly shapeless in his bell-sleeved nightgown,
one sprite blows a spritely prelude
on a tilted trumpet, pitched
too high for the earthier folk
to catch. But the birch queen's smiling, she conducts him
with outstretched arms and a length of nonchalant scarf.
Two others dance till their sly, sensual faces
break with the dirty laugh
of a night just round the corner.
In the grass, the copper-plated
leaves are magically turning
to buds of wheat. The birches
stagger on coltish legs, their heads replete
with magpies, Fabergé eggs
and other astonishing brainwaves.